Everyday Success™
First Grade

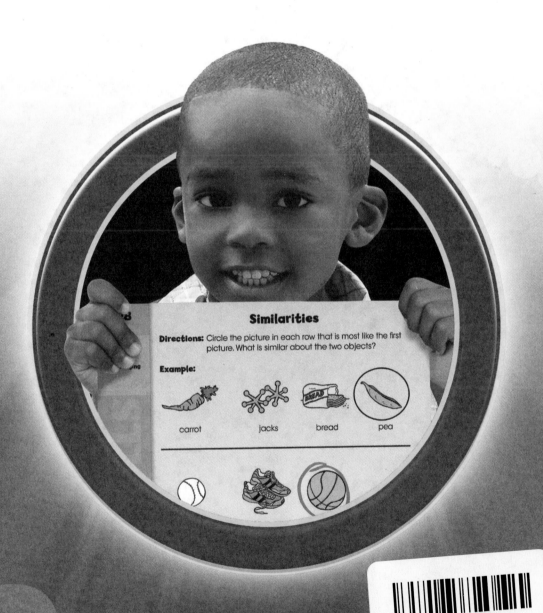

Similarities

Directions: Circle the picture in each row that is most like the first picture. What is similar about the two objects?

Example:

carrot   jacks   bread   pea

THINKING KIDS™

P.O. Box 35665 • Greensboro, NC 27425 USA
carsondellosa.com

Thinking Kids™
An imprint of Carson-Dellosa Publishing LLC
P.O. Box 35665
Greensboro, NC 27425 USA

ISBN 978-1-4838-1312-7

02-072157784

Table of Contents

INTRODUCTION

Everyday Success First Grade

Welcome to the *Everyday Success* series!

Building a strong foundation is an essential part of your child's everyday success. This series features a variety of activity pages that make learning fun, keeping your child engaged and entertained at the same time. These colorful workbooks will help children meet important proficiency standards with activities that strengthen their basic skills, math, and reading.

With the *Everyday Success* series, learning isn't just contained to the pages of the workbook. Each activity offers "One Step Further," a suggestion for children to continue the learning activity on their own. This encourages children to take what they've learned and apply it to everyday situations, reinforcing their comprehension of the activity while exploring the world around them, preparing them with the skills needed to succeed in the 21st century.

These books provide an outstanding educational experience and important learning tools to prepare your child for the future. The *Everyday Success* series offers hours of educational entertainment that will make your child want to come back for more!

Basic Skills

Rhyming Words

Rhyming words are words that sound alike at the end of the word. **Cat** and **hat** rhyme.

Directions: Draw a circle around each word pair that rhymes. Draw an **X** on each pair that does **not** rhyme.

Example:

soap
rope

red
dog

book
hook

cold
rock

cat
hat

yellow
black

one
two

rock
sock

rat
flat

good
nice

you
to

meet
toy

old
sold

sale
whale

word
letter

One Step Further

Choose two rhyming words from this page.
Can you find both objects in your home?

Rhyming Words

Rhyming words are words that sound alike at the end of the word.

Directions: Draw a line to match the pictures that rhyme. Write two of your rhyming word pairs below.

Sasha   Masha

Tasha   C

One Step Further
What word rhymes with your name?
Make up a word if you have to!

Everyday Success First Grade

ABC Order

Directions: Circle the first letter of each word. Then, put each pair of the words in **ABC** order.

ⓒar   ⓑird   moon   two   nest   fan

bird   Fan   Nest

car   Moon   Two

card   dog   pig   bike   sun   pie

bike   dog   pig

card   pie   sun

One Step Further
Write three words. Ask a friend to put them in ABC order.

ABC Order

Directions: Look at the words in each box. Circle the word that comes first in **ABC** order.

duck
four
rock

chair
apple
yellow

peach
this
walk

game
boy
pink

light
come
one

mouse
ten
orange

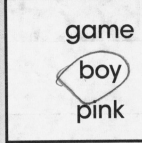

angel
table
hair

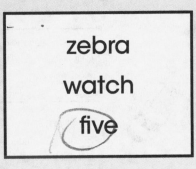

zebra
watch
five

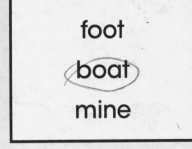

foot
boat
mine

look
blue
rope

who
dog
black

book
tan
six

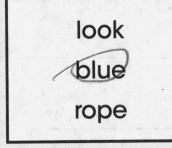

One Step Further
Write down names of your friends and family.
Can you put them in ABC order?

Everyday Success First Grade

Compound Words

Compound words are two words that are put together to make one new word.

Directions: Look at the pictures and the two words that are next to each other. Put the words together to make a new word. Write the new word.

Example:

house + boat =

houseboat

side + walk =

si dewalk

lip + stick =

lipstick

lunch + box =

lunch box

One Step Further
What is your favorite food to pack in
your lunchbox?

Compound Words

Directions: Circle the compound word that completes each sentence. Write each word on the lines.

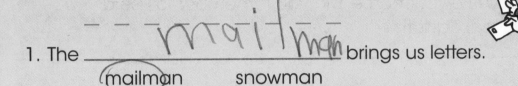

1. The _____ _mailman_ brings us letters.

   (mailman)   snowman

2. A _____ _sunflower_ grows tall.

   sunlight   (sunflower)

3. The snow falls _____ _outside_.

   (outside)   inside

4. A _____ _raindrop_ fell on my head.

   raindrop   rainbow

5. I put the letter in a _____ _mailbox_.

   mailbox   shoebox

One Step Further

Write a letter to a friend. Put it in the mailbox or give it to the mailman to send.

Names

You are a special person. Your name begins with a capital letter. We put a capital letter at the beginning of people's names because they are special.

Directions: Write your name. Did you remember to use a capital letter?

Asha

Directions: Write each person's name. Use a capital letter at the beginning.

 Ted _Ted_

 Katie _Katie_

 Mike _Mike_

 Tim _Tim_

One Step Further
Write the names of your family members.
How many people are in your family?

Days of the Week

The days of the week begin with capital letters.

Directions: Write the days of the week in the spaces below. Put them in order. Be sure to start with capital letters.

Tuesday

Saturday

Monday

Friday

Thursday

Sunday

Wednesday

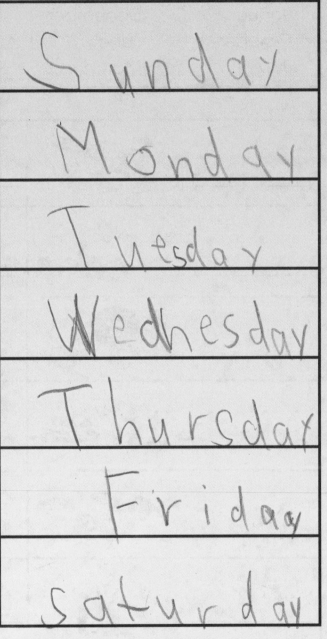

Sunday

Monday

Tuesday

Wednesday

Thursday

Friday

saturday

One Step Further
What is your favorite day of the week?
What do you like about it?

Months of the Year

The months of the year begin with capital letters.

Directions: Write the months of the year in order on the calendar below. Be sure to start with capital letters.

January	December	April	May
October	June	September	February
July	March	November	August

January

February

March

April

May

June

July

August

september

October

November

December

One Step Further

What month were you born in? Do you know anyone else born in that month?

More Than One

Directions: An **s** at the end of a word often means there is more than one. Look at each picture. Circle the correct word. Write the word on the line.

two | four | one
dog   dogs | flower   flowers | bikes   bike

dogs   _flowers_   _bike_

three | a | two
toys   toy | lamb   lambs | cat   cats

Toys   _lamb_   _cats_

One Step Further
Name something you own more than one of.
How many do you own of that object?

BASIC SKILLS

More Than One

Directions: Read the nouns under the pictures. Then, write each noun under **One** or **More Than One**.

One

barn wagon

horse

barn   cows

ducks

wagon

horse

pigs

More Than One

cows ducks

pigs

One Step Further

Look around the room for a book. Do you see one book, or more than one book?

BASIC SKILLS

More Than One

Directions: Choose the word that completes each sentence. Write each word on the line.

1. I have a __dog__.

       dog   dogs

2. Four __apples__ are on the tree.

      apple   apples

3. I read two __books__ today.

      book   books

4. My __bike__ is blue.

      bike   bikes

5. We saw lots of __monkeys__ at the zoo.

      monkey   monkeys

One Step Further

Look in your closet. What do you see more than one of?

Everyday Success First Grade

Riddles

Directions: Draw a line from the riddle to the animal it tells about.

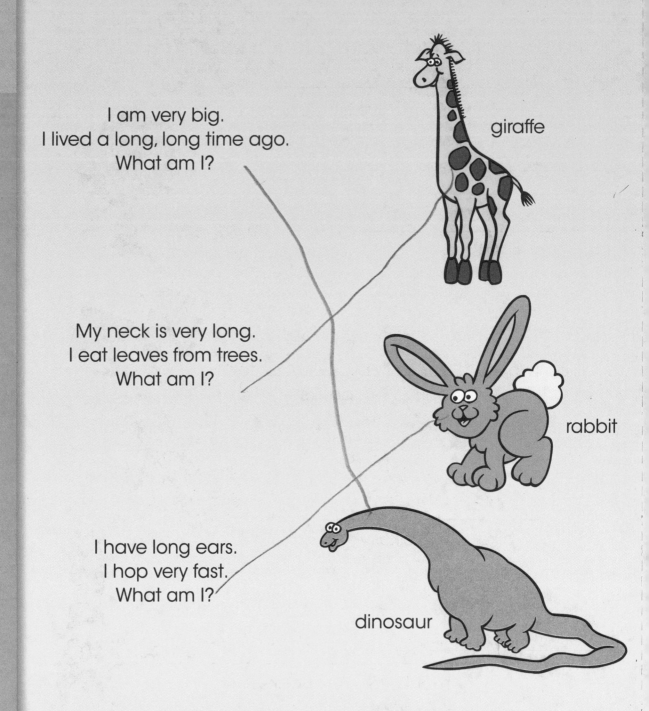

I am very big.
I lived a long, long time ago.
What am I?

giraffe

My neck is very long.
I eat leaves from trees.
What am I?

rabbit

I have long ears.
I hop very fast.
What am I?

dinosaur

One Step Further
Tell a riddle about another animal.
See if a friend can guess the animal.

Riddles

Directions: Read the word and write it on the line. Then, read each riddle and draw a line from the riddle to the picture it tells about.

house

house

kitten

kitten

flower

flower

pony

pony

I like to play.
I am little. I am soft.
What am I?

house

I am big.
You live in me.
What am I?

kitten

I am pretty.
I am green and yellow.
What am I?

pony

I can jump. I can run.
I am brown.
What am I?

flower

One Step Further
How else could you describe a kitten?
How else could you describe a flower?

Riddles

Directions: Write a word from the box to answer each riddle.

sundae	book	chair	sun

There are many words in me.
I am fun to read.
What am I?

book

I am soft and yellow.
You can sit on me.
What am I?

chair

I am in the sky in the day.
I am hot. I am yellow.
What am I?

sun

I am cold. I am sweet.
You like to eat me.
What am I?

sundae

One Step Further
Choose an object at school.
Describe the object and ask a friend to guess.

These Keep Me Warm

Directions: Color the things that keep you warm.

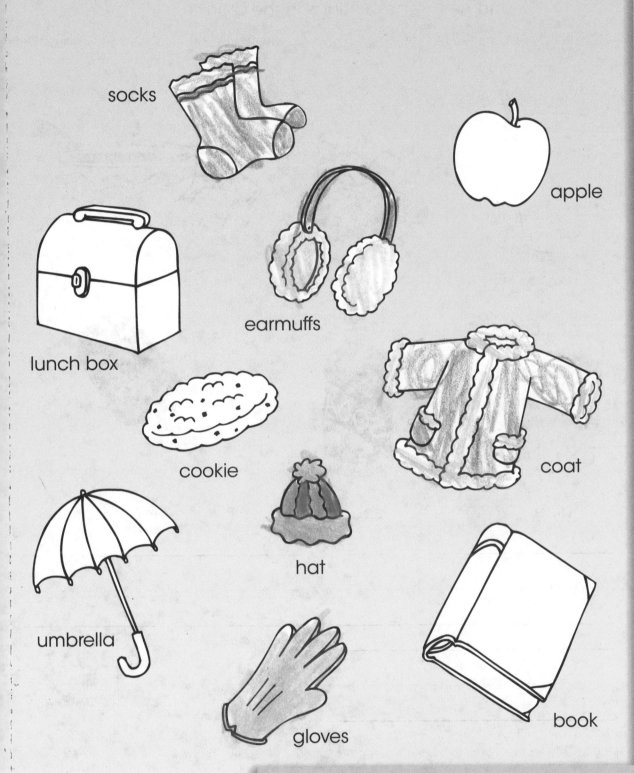

socks

apple

lunch box

earmuffs

cookie

coat

umbrella

hat

gloves

book

One Step Further

What do you do when you are cold?

What clothes do you wear during the winter?

Things to Drink

Directions: Circle the pictures of things you can drink. Write the names of those things in the blanks.

milk ice soup and crackers

juice soda ice-cream bar

_____   _____
Juice   soda
_____   _____
milk

One Step Further
Name something else you can drink.
What is your favorite thing to drink?

Vocabulary

Directions: Read the words. Trace and write them on the lines. Look at each picture. Write **hot** or **cold** on the lines to show if it is hot or cold.

hot   hot   hot

cold   cold   cold

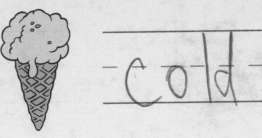

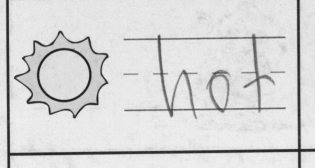

 ☀	hot	 🍦	cold
 ⛄	cold	 ☕	hot

One Step Further
What foods are hot? What foods are cold?
Which of these foods do you like best?

BASIC SKILLS

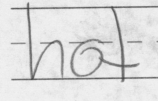

Classifying

Everyday Success First Grade

Vocabulary

Classifying

Directions: Read the words. Trace and write them on the lines. Look at each picture. Write **day** or **night** on the lines to show if they happen during the day or night.

day day day

night night night

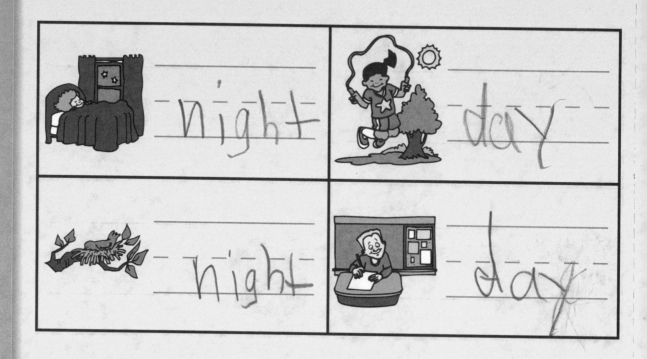

night

day

night

day

One Step Further
What do you do during the day?
What do you do at night?

Night and Day

Directions: Write the words from the box under the pictures they describe.

stars	sun	moon	rays	dark	light	night	day

stars, ~~moon~~

light, days

moon, dark,

rays, sun

night,

One Step Further

How do you know when it's nighttime?
Describe how you can tell.

Clowns and Balloons

Some words describe clowns. Some words describe balloons.

Directions: Read the words. Write the words that match in the correct columns.

| float | laughs | hat | string | air | feet | pop | nose |

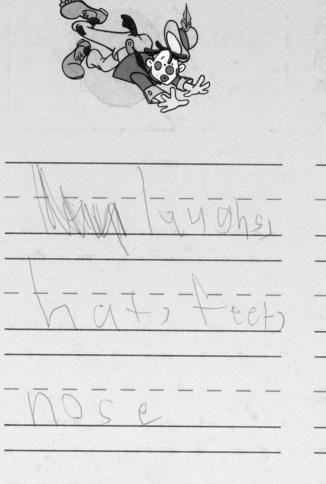

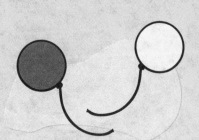

laughs

hat, feet

nose

Floats

air, pop

string

One Step Further

How else could you describe a clown?
Tell a story about a clown to a friend.

Similarities

Directions: Circle the picture in each row that is most like the first picture. What is similar about the two objects?

Example:

potato

rose

tomato

tree

shirt

mittens

boots

jacket

tiger

giraffe

lion

zebra

One Step Further
Find two objects in your room that go together. Describe their similarities.

Everyday Success First Grade

Similarities

Directions: Circle the picture in each row that is most like the first picture. What is similar about the two objects?

Example:

carrot   jacks   bread   pea

baseball   sneakers   basketball   bat

store   school   home   bakery

One Step Further

What is your favorite store?
Name another store that is similar.

Food Groups

Directions: Color the meats and eggs **brown**. Color the fruits and vegetables **green**. Color the breads **tan**. Color the dairy foods (milk and cheese) **yellow**.

fish

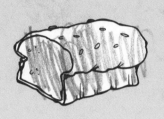

bread

apple

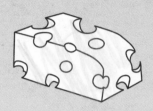

cheese

crackers

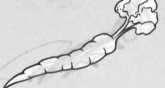

carrot

orange

eggs

steaks

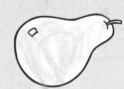

pear

milk

yogurt

ice cream

chicken

potato

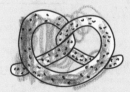

pretzel

One Step Further
What is your favorite food from each of these food groups?

Everyday Success First Grade

Things That Belong Together

Directions: Circle the pictures in each row that belong together.

Row 1   cookies   cake   beans   ice cream

Row 2   kite   dice   checkers   chess

Directions: Write the names of the things that do **not** belong.
Why do these pictures not belong?

Row 1   beans

Row 2   kite

One Step Further
Name a game you can play on a rainy day.
Draw it here.

What Does Not Belong?

Directions: Draw an **X** on the picture that does **not** belong in each group.

fruit

apple   peach   corn   watermelon

wild animals

bear   kitten   gorilla   lion

flowers

grass   rose   daisy   tulip

One Step Further
Name another object that belongs in each category on this page. Draw the objects.

Everyday Success First Grade

What Does Not Belong?

Classifying

Directions: Draw an **X** on the word in each row that does **not** belong.

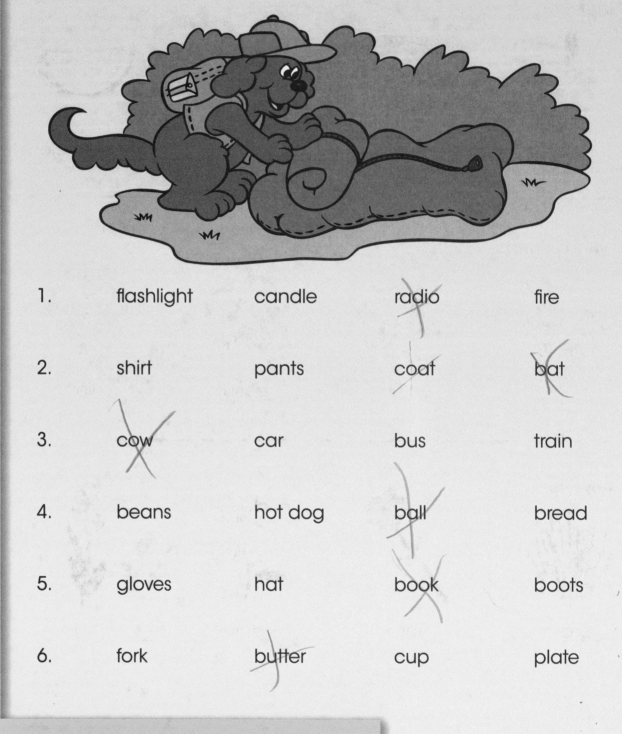

1.   flashlight   candle   ~~radio~~   fire

2.   shirt   pants   ~~coat~~   ~~bat~~

3.   ~~cow~~   car   bus   train

4.   beans   hot dog   ~~ball~~   bread

5.   gloves   hat   ~~book~~   boots

6.   fork   ~~butter~~   cup   plate

One Step Further
Tell a story about a camping trip.
Make up characters for your story.

Things That Belong Together

Directions: Circle the pictures in each row that belong together.

| Row 1 | knife | key | fork | spoon |

| Row 2 | orange | apple | candy | banana |

Directions: Write the names of the pictures that do **not** belong. Why do these pictures not belong?

Row 1   key

Row 2   candy

One Step Further
What is your favorite fruit? Draw it here.
Which row does it belong in?

Everyday Success First Grade

Why They Are Different

Directions: Look at your answers on page 33. Write why each object does not belong.

_____

- - - - - - - - - - - - - - - - - - - -

Row 1 _____

_____

- - - - - - - - - - - - - - - - - - - -

Row 2 _____

Directions: For each object, draw a group of pictures that belong with it.

candy bar

lettuce

One Step Further
Look through your bookbag and choose an item. What other items go with it?

What Does Not Belong?

Directions: Circle the two things that do not belong in the picture. Write why they do not belong.

1. _Because_ _____

2. _____

One Step Further
Describe what is happening in the picture.
What winter activities do you enjoy?

Color Code Classifying

Directions: Underline **name words** in **blue**. Underline **number words** in **red**. Underline **animal words** in **yellow**. Underline **color words** in **green**.

pig	Kim	dog	blue	red	green
ten	five	Jack	two	cow	Lee

Directions: Write each word on the correct line.

Name Words

_____   _____   _____

- - - - - - - - -   - - - - - - - - -   - - - - - - - - -

_____   _____   _____

Number Words

_____   _____   _____

- - - - - - - - -   - - - - - - - - -   - - - - - - - - -

_____   _____   _____

Animal Words

_____   _____   _____

- - - - - - - - -   - - - - - - - - -   - - - - - - - - -

_____   _____   _____

Color Words

_____   _____   _____

- - - - - - - - -   - - - - - - - - -   - - - - - - - - -

_____   _____   _____

One Step Further

What other words go in these categories?
List them on another sheet of paper.

Classifying

Menu Mix-Up

Directions: Circle names of **drinks** in red.
Circle names of **vegetables** in green.
Circle names of **desserts** in pink.

water

cookie

juice

corn

peas

milk

pie

carrot

cake

Directions: Write each food word on the correct line.

Drinks	Vegetables	Desserts

One Step Further
Pretend you own a restaurant.
What would be on your menu?

Word Sort

Directions: Circle words that name **colors** in **red**.
Circle words that name **shapes** in **yellow**.
Circle words that name **numbers** in **green**.

five   blue

ten

circle

square   nine   purple

triangle   brown

Directions: Write each word on the correct line.

Colors	Shapes	Numbers

One Step Further
Sort your clothes based on color.
What color is the biggest group?

BASIC SKILLS

Where Does It Belong?

Directions: Read the words.
Draw a **circle** around the **sky words**.
Draw a **line** under the **land words**.
Draw a **box** around the **sea words**.

city 	rabbit	planet 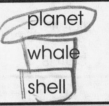
cloud	forest	whale
shark	moon	shell

Directions: Write each word on the correct line.

Sky Words

cloud   moon   planet

Land Words

Sea Words

One Step Further
Walk around your neighborhood.
What other land words could you add?

Classification

Directions: The words in each box form a group. Choose the word from the box that describes each group and write it on the line.

clothes	family	colors
flowers	fruits	animals
coins	toys	noises

rose
buttercup
tulip
daisy

_____

crash
bang
ring
pop

_____

mother
father
sister
brother

_____

puzzle
wagon
blocks
doll

_____

green
purple
blue
red

_____

grapes
orange
apple
plum

_____

shirt
socks
dress
coat

_____

dime
penny
nickel
quarter

_____

dog
horse
elephant
moose

_____

One Step Further

Look in your closet or drawer. What other words could be classified as clothes?

Things That Go Together

Directions: Draw a line to connect the things that go together.

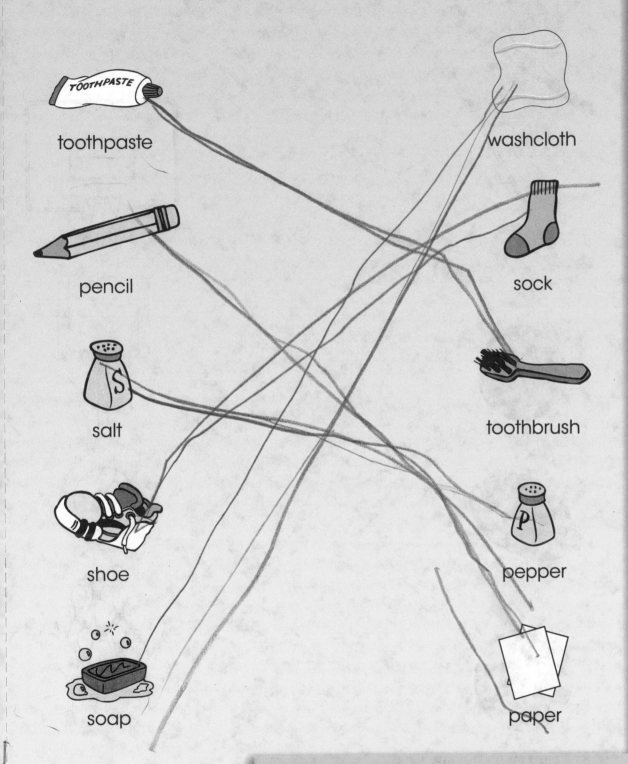

toothpaste

washcloth

pencil

sock

salt

toothbrush

shoe

pepper

soap

paper

One Step Further
Look around your home.
Find two more things that go together.

Things That Go Together

Directions: Draw a line to connect the things that go together.

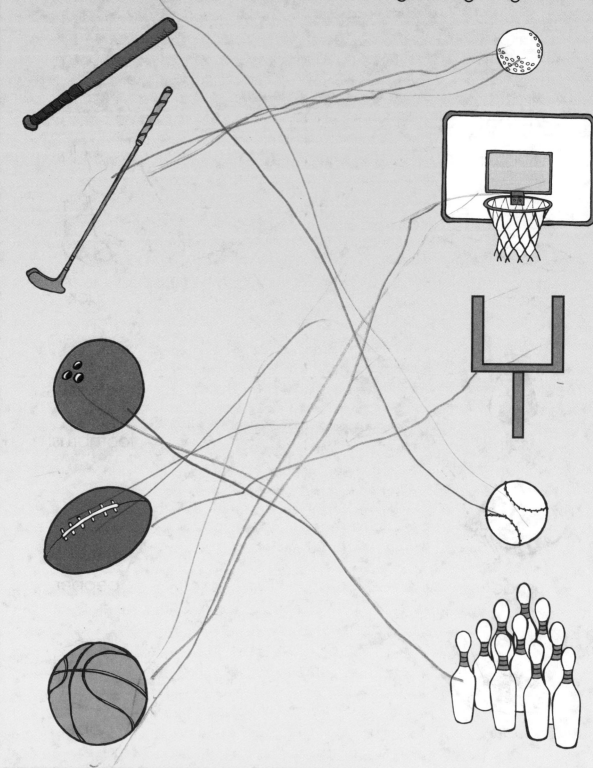

One Step Further
What is your favorite sport to play?
What do you like about it?

Raking Leaves

Directions: Write a number in each box to show the order of the story.

One Step Further
Go outside and find 10 leaves.
What color are the leaves?

Everyday Success First Grade

Make a Snowman!

Directions: Write the number of the sentence that goes with each picture in the box.

1. Roll a large snowball for the snowman's bottom.
2. Make another snowball and put it on top of the first.
3. Put the last snowball on top.
4. Dress the snowman.

One Step Further
Tell a story about building a snowman.
Have you ever built a snowman?

How Flowers Grow

Directions: Read the story. Then, write the steps to grow a flower.

First, find a sunny spot. Then, plant the seed. Water it. The flower will start to grow. Pull the weeds around it. Remember to keep giving the flower water. Enjoy your flower.

1. _____.

2. _____.

3. _____.

4. _____.

5. _____.

One Step Further
What is your favorite flower? Draw a picture of a beautiful garden full of flowers.

Same and Different

Reading to find out how things are alike or different can help you picture and remember what you read. Things that are alike are called **similarities**. Things that are not alike are called **differences**.

Similarity: Beth and Michelle are both girls.
Difference: Beth has short hair, but Michelle has long hair.

Directions: Read the story.

Michelle and Beth are wearing new dresses. Both dresses are striped and have four shiny buttons. Each dress has a belt and a pocket. Beth's dress is blue and white, while Michelle's is yellow and white. The stripes on Beth's dress go up and down. Stripes on Michelle's dress go from side to side. Beth's pocket is bigger with room for a kitten.

Directions: Add the details. Color the dresses. Show how the dresses are alike and how they are different.

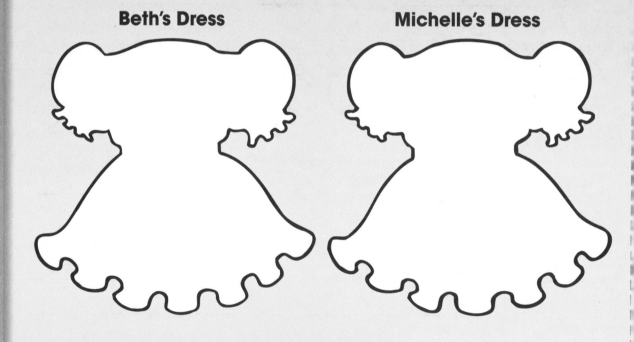

Beth's Dress   **Michelle's Dress**

One Step Further
Sit with a friend. Make a list of your similarities and differences.

Comparing Cars

Directions: Read the story.

Sarah built a car for a race. Sarah's car has wheels, a steering wheel, and a place to sit just like the family car. It doesn't have a motor, a key, or a gas pedal. Sarah came in second in last year's race. This year, she hopes to win the race.

Directions: Write **S** beside the things Sarah's car has that are like things the family car has. Write **D** beside the things that are different.

_____

_____

_____

_____

_____

_____

_____

 steering wheel

 motor

 gas pedal

 seat

 wheels

One Step Further
Make a list of other things a family car would have.

Everyday Success First Grade

Color the Path

Directions: Color the path the girl should take to go home. Use the sentences to help you.

1. Go to the school and turn left.
2. At the end of the street, turn right.
3. Walk past the park and turn right.
4. After you pass the pool, turn right.

One Step Further

Create a map of your neighborhood.
Be sure to label your house and your street!

Following Directions

Directions: Look at the pictures. Follow the directions in each box.

Draw a circle around the caterpillar. Draw a line under the stick.

Draw an **X** on the mother bird. Draw a triangle around the baby birds.

Draw a box around the rabbit.

Color the flowers. Count the bees. There are _____ bees.

One Step Further
Draw a flower for a friend. Give your friend directions on how to color the flower.

Fun With Directions

Directions: Follow the number code to color the balloons. Color the clown, too.

1 — **blue**   2 — orange   3 — yellow   4 — **green**   5 — **purple**

6 — **brown**   7 — red   8 — gray   9 — tan   10 — pink

One Step Further

What is your favorite color balloon?
Draw a square around that balloon.

Draw With Directions

Directions: Follow the directions to complete the picture.

1. Draw a smiling yellow face on the sun.

2. Color the fish **blue**. Draw two more **blue** fish in the water.

3. Draw a **brown** bird under the cloud. Draw **blue** raindrops under the cloud.

4. Color the boat **red**. Color one sail pink. Color the other sail **green**.

5. Color the starfish orange. Draw two more orange starfish.

One Step Further
Tell a story about a day at the beach.
Make up characters for your story.

Everyday Success First Grade

Directions for Decorating

Directions: Follow the directions to decorate the bedroom.

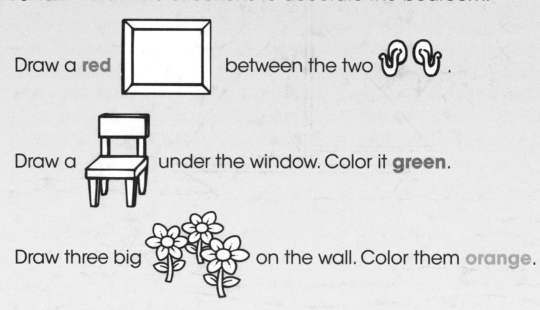

Draw a **red** [frame] between the two [hooks].

Draw a [chair] under the window. Color it **green**.

Draw three big [flowers] on the wall. Color them **orange**.

Draw a picture of something you would like to have in your bedroom.

One Step Further
How is your room decorated?
How would you like to decorate your room?

BASIC SKILLS

Following Directions

Read the sentences. Then, follow the directions.

Directions: Jared is making a snowman. He needs your help. Draw a **black** hat on the snowman. Draw **red** buttons. Now, draw a **green** scarf. Draw a happy face on the snowman.

One Step Further
What else would you see on a snowy winter day? Draw it in the picture.

Everyday Success First Grade

Following Directions

Follow the directions to make a paper sack puppet.

Directions: Find a small sack that fits your hand. Cut out teeth from colored paper. Glue them on the sack. Cut out ears. Glue them on the sack. Cut out eyes, a nose, and a tongue. Glue them all on.

Directions: Number the pictures **1**, **2**, **3**, and **4** to show the correct order.

One Step Further
Make a paper sack puppet with a friend.
Put on a puppet show!

Draw a Tiger

Directions: Follow directions to complete the picture of the tiger.

1. Draw **black** stripes on the tiger's body and tail.

2. Color the tiger's tongue **red**.

3. Draw claws on the feet.

4. Draw a **black** nose and two **black** eyes on the tiger's face.

5. Color the rest of the tiger **orange**.

6. Draw tall, **green** grass for the tiger to sleep in.

One Step Further
What is your favorite animal?
What steps do you take to draw this animal?

Everyday Success First Grade

Color Names

Directions: Trace the letters to write the name of each color. Then, write the name again by yourself.

Example:

orange   orange

blue

green

yellow

red

brown

BASIC SKILLS

One Step Further

Find an object in your home that matches each color on this page.

Color Names: Sentences

Directions: Use the color words to complete these sentences. Then, put a period at the end.

Example: My new are **orange.**

green tree

blue bike

yellow chick

red ball

1. The baby is ___yellow___

2. This  is ___green___

3. My  is big and ___red___

4. My sister's  is ___blue___

One Step Further
Make up a sentence of your own. Include at least one color word.

Animal Names

Directions: Fill in the missing letters for each word.

Example:

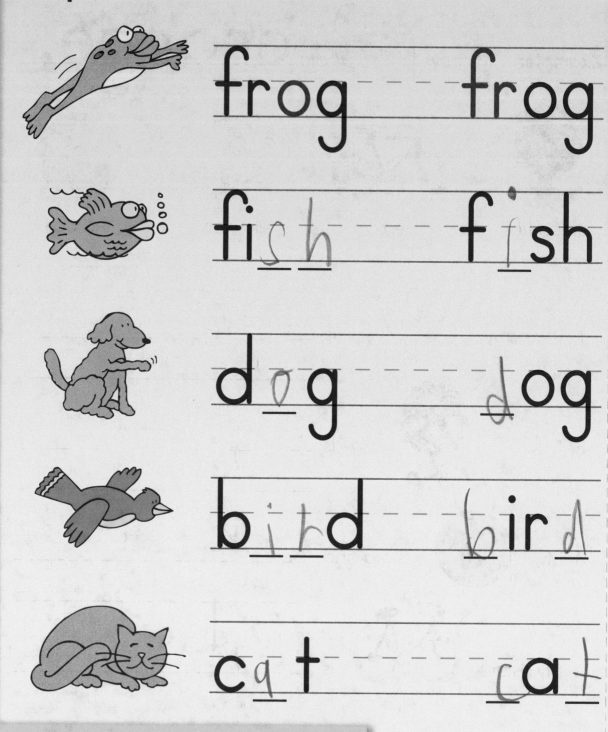

frog   frog

fish   fish

dog   dog

bird   bird

cat   cat

One Step Further
Draw another animal. Write the name of
the animal.

Animal Names: Sentences

A **sentence** tells about something.

Directions: These sentences tell about animals. Write the word that completes each sentence.

Example:

_____

My _____ jumps high.

_____

1. I take my _____ for a walk.

_____

2. My _____ lives in water.

_____

3. My _____ can sing.

_____

4. My _____ has a long tail.

One Step Further
Do you have any pets? Make up a sentence about your pet or another animal.

Everyday Success First Grade

Things That Go

Directions: Trace the letters to write the name of each thing. Write each name again by yourself. Then, color the pictures.

Example:

 car   car

 truck

 train

 plane

 bike

One Step Further

How many of these things have you ridden on? What is your favorite way to travel?

Things That Go: Sentences

Directions: These sentences tell about things that go. Write the word that completes each sentence.

Example:

The __car__ is in the garage.

1. The __truck__ was at the farm.

2. My __bike__ had a flat tire.

3. The __plane__ flew high.

4. The __train__ went fast.

One Step Further
Write another sentence about the car you see on this page. What color is the car?

Everyday Success First Grade

Clothing Words

Spelling

Directions: Trace the letters to write the name of each clothing word. Then, write each name again by yourself.

Example:

shirt   shirt

pants

jacket

socks

shoes

dress

One Step Further
Describe the clothing you are wearing right now.

Clothing Words: Sentences

Directions: Some of these sentences tell a whole idea. Others have something missing. If something is missing, draw a line to the word that completes the sentence. Put a period at the end of each sentence.

Example:

She is wearing a polka-dot

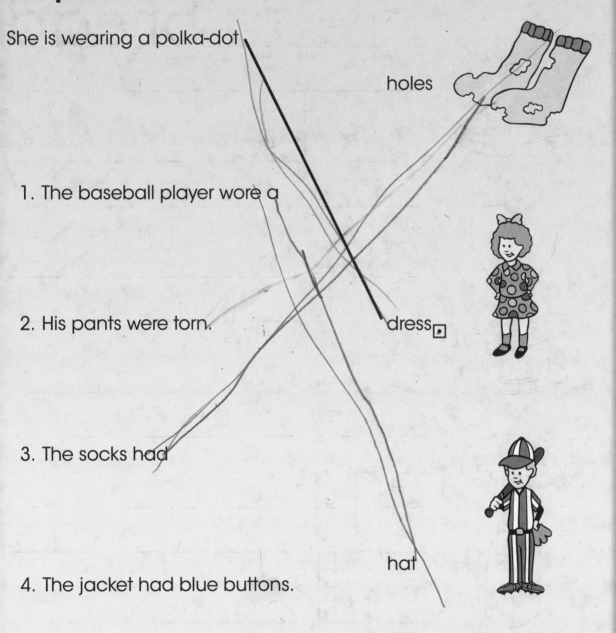

holes

1. The baseball player wore a

2. His pants were torn.

dress.

3. The socks had

hat

4. The jacket had blue buttons.

One Step Further
Write a sentence about your favorite article of clothing.

Food Names

Directions: Trace the letters to write the name of each food word. Write each name again by yourself. Then, color the pictures.

Example:

 bread bread

 cookie

 apple

 cake

 egg

 milk

 One Step Further
Which of these foods have you eaten most recently? Which is your favorite?

Food Names: Asking Sentences

An **asking sentence** asks a question. Asking sentences end with a question mark.

Directions: Write each sentence on the line. Begin each sentence with a capital letter. Put a period at the end of the telling sentences and a question mark at the end of the asking sentences.

Example: do you like cake

Do you like cake?

1. the cow has spots

2. is that cookie good

3. she ate the apple

One Step Further
Write an asking sentence to a friend.
What is your friend's answer?

Number Words

Directions: Trace the letters to write the name of each number.
Then, color the number pictures.

1 one   2 two

3 three   4 four

5 five   6 six

7 seven   8 eight

9 nine   10 ten

One Step Further
How old are you? Circle that number.
Draw a birthday cake with candles.

Number Words: Asking Sentences

Directions: Use a number word to answer each question.

| one | five | seven | three | eight |

1. How many trees are there?

_____

- - - - - - - - - - - - - -

_____

2. How many flowers are there?

_____

- - - - - - - - - - - - - -

_____

3. How many presents are there?

_____

- - - - - - - - - - - - - -

_____

4. How many clocks are there?

_____

- - - - - - - - - - - - - -

_____

5. How many forks are there?

_____

- - - - - - - - - - - - - -

_____

One Step Further

How many lamps are in your bedroom?
How many clocks are in your bedroom?

Action Words

Action words tell things we can do.

Directions: Trace the letters to write each action word. Then, write the action word again by yourself.

Example:

sleep sleep

run

make

ride

play

stop

One Step Further
What other action words can you think of?
Do those actions.

Action Words: More Than One

To show more than one of something, add **s** to the end of the word.

Example: one cat  two cats

Directions: In each sentence, add **s** to show more than one. Then, write the action word that completes each sentence.

Example: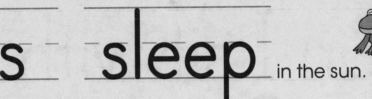

The frog ___ **s** ___ **sleep** ___ in the sun.

sit	jump	stop	ride

1. The boy _____ _____ on the fence.

2. The car _____ _____ at the sign.

3. The girl _____ _____ in the water.

4. The dog _____ _____ in the wagon.

One Step Further
Think of a friend. Write a sentence about something you and your friend do together.

Everyday Success First Grade

Action Words: Asking Sentences

Directions: Write an asking sentence about each picture. Begin each sentence with **can**. Add an action word. Begin each asking sentence with a capital letter and end it with a question mark.

Example: I with you can

Can I sit with you?

1. she can

2. with you can I

3. can she fast

One Step Further
How fast can you run?
Ask an adult to time you.

Sense Words

Directions: Circle the word that is spelled correctly. Then, write the correct spelling in the blank.

Example:

tast
(taste)
tste

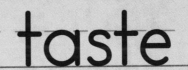

touch
tuch
touh

smel
smll
smell

her
hear
har

see
se
sea

One Step Further
Ask a friend to name another word.
Do you know how to spell that word?

Everyday Success First Grade

Sense Words: Sentences

Directions: Read each sentence and write the correct words in the blanks.

Example:

taste   mouth

I can _____ **taste** _____ things with my _____ **mouth** _____.

touch   hands

1. I can _____ things with my _____.

smell   nose

2. I can _____ things with my _____.

hear   ears

3. I can _____ with my _____.

see   eyes

4. I can _____ things with my _____.

One Step Further
Which sense do you use the most?
Which do you think you use the least? Why?

BASIC SKILLS

Beginning Sounds

Directions: Say the sound of the letter at the beginning of each row. Find the pictures in each row that begin with the same letter. Write the letter under the pictures.

Example:

s _____ S _____ S _____ _____

w _____ _____ _____ _____

c _____ _____ _____ _____

p _____ _____ _____ _____

s _____ _____ _____ _____

r _____ _____ _____ _____

One Step Further
Name another object that starts with the **Ss** sound.

Spelling

Weather Words: Sentences

Directions: Write the weather word that completes each sentence. Put a period at the end of the telling sentences and a question mark at the end of the asking sentences.

Example:

Do flowers grow in the _____ sun _____ ?

rain	water	wet	hot

1. The sun makes me _____ hot _____

2. When it rains, the grass gets _____ wet _____

3. Do you think it will _____ rain _____ on our picnic

4. Should you drink the _____ water _____ from the rain

One Step Further

What is the weather like right now?
Write a sentence about it.

My World

Directions: Fill in the missing letters for each word.

tree  tree

grass grass

flower  flower

pond  pond

sand  sand

sky  sky

One Step Further
Look outside. How many of the objects on this page can you see?

Everyday Success First Grade

My World

Directions: The letters in the words below are mixed up. Unscramble the letters and write each word correctly.

 etre tree

 srags grass

 loefwr flower

 dnop pond

 dnsa sand

 yks sky

One Step Further
Draw a picture of a summer day. Include all of the objects you see on this page.

My World: Sentences

Directions: Write the word that completes each sentence. Put a period at the end of the telling sentences and a question mark at the end of the asking sentences.

Example:

Does the sun shine on the ___flowers___?

tree	grass	pond	sky

1. The ___sky___ was full of dark clouds

2. Can you climb the ___tree___

3. Did you see the duck in the ___pond___

4. The ___grass___ in the yard was tall

One Step Further
Write a sentence about the world around you. Think about your state and your country.

The Parts of My Body: Sentences

Directions: Write the word that completes each sentence. Put a period at the end of the telling sentences and a question mark at the end of the asking sentences.

Example:

I wear my hat on my _head_.

arms	legs	feet	hands

1. How strong are your _arms_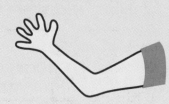

2. You wear shoes on your _feet_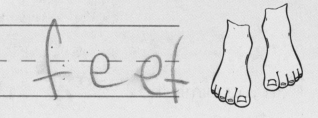

3. If you're happy and you know it, clap your _hand_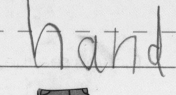

4. My pants covered my _legs_

One Step Further
Name another article of clothing you wear on your feet. What is on your feet right now?

The Parts of My Body: Sentences

Directions: Read the sentence parts below. Draw a line from the first part of the sentence to the second part that completes it.

1. I give big hugs   with my arms.

                             with my car.

2. My feet   drive the car.

                             got wet in the rain.

3. I have a bump   on my head.

                             on my coat.

4. My mittens   keep my arms warm.

                             keep my hands warm.

5. I can jump high   using my legs.

                             using a spoon.

One Step Further
What can you do with your arms?
What can you do with your legs?

Everyday Success First Grade

The Parts of My Body: Sentences

Directions: Read the two sentences on each line and draw a line between them. Then, write each sentence again on the lines below. Begin each sentence with a capital letter, and end each one with a period or a question mark.

Example: wash your hands|they are dirty

Wash your hands.
They are dirty.

1. you have big arms are you very strong

_____

_____

_____

2. I have two feet I can run fast

_____

_____

_____

One Step Further
Write two different sentences about your hands.

Math

MATH

Addition

Putting numbers together is called **addition**. When you add two numbers together, you get a **total**, or **sum**. The symbol used for addition is called a **plus sign (+)**. The symbol used for a total is an **equal sign (=)**.

Directions: Follow the instructions below to create and solve the addition problems.

One pony is eating hay.	Draw one more pony in this box.	Write the total number of ponies.

 +  =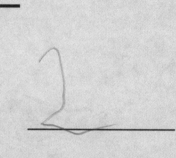

One lamb is jumping.	Draw two more lambs in this box.	Write the total number of lambs.

 +  =

One Step Further
Pretend you own one book. You are given two more books. How many do you have now?

MATH

Addition

Directions: Count the shapes and write the numbers below to tell how many in all.

1 + 1 = 2

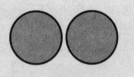 

2 + 1 = 3

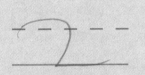 

1 + 2 = 3

 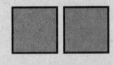 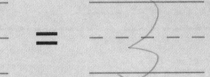

3 + 1 = 4

One Step Further
How many square objects can you find in your bedroom? Count them.

Everyday Success First Grade

MATH

Sums 0 to 3

Directions: Add.

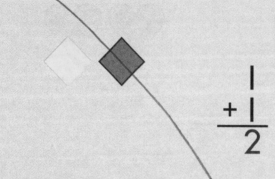

$$\begin{array}{r} 1 \\ +1 \\ \hline 2 \end{array}$$

$2 + 1 = \underline{3}$

$$\begin{array}{r} 2 \\ +1 \\ \hline 3 \end{array}$$

$$\begin{array}{r} 1 \\ +2 \\ \hline 3 \end{array}$$

$1 + 1 = \underline{2}$

$1 + 2 = \underline{3}$

$2 + 0 = \underline{2}$

$$\begin{array}{r} 2 \\ +0 \\ \hline 2 \end{array}$$

$3 + 0 = \underline{3}$

$$\begin{array}{r} 3 \\ +0 \\ \hline 3 \end{array}$$

$0 + 2 = \underline{2}$

$$\begin{array}{r} 0 \\ +2 \\ \hline 2 \end{array}$$

$0 + 3 = \underline{2}$

$$\begin{array}{r} 0 \\ +3 \\ \hline 3 \end{array}$$

$$\begin{array}{r} 0 \\ +0 \\ \hline 0 \end{array}$$

$1 + 0 = \underline{1}$

$$\begin{array}{r} 1 \\ +0 \\ \hline 1 \end{array}$$

$$\begin{array}{r} 0 \\ +1 \\ \hline 1 \end{array}$$

$0 + 0 = \underline{0}$

$0 + 1 = \underline{1}$

One Step Further
Find two pencils. Find one crayon.
Add how many objects there are.

Sums of 4 and 5

Directions: Add.

$$\begin{array}{r} 4 \\ +1 \\ \hline 5 \end{array}$$

$4 + 1 = \underline{\quad 5 \quad}$

$$\begin{array}{r} 1 \\ +4 \\ \hline 5 \end{array}$$

$1 + 4 = \underline{\quad 5 \quad}$

$$\begin{array}{r} 2 \\ +3 \\ \hline \end{array}$$

$2 + 3 = \underline{\quad 5 \quad}$

$$\begin{array}{r} 3 \\ +2 \\ \hline \end{array}$$

$3 + 2 = \underline{\quad 5 \quad}$

$$\begin{array}{r} 2 \\ +2 \\ \hline \end{array}$$

$2 + 2 = \underline{\quad 4 \quad}$

$$\begin{array}{r} 4 \\ +0 \\ \hline \end{array}$$

$4 + 0 = \underline{\quad 4 \quad}$

$$\begin{array}{r} 0 \\ +4 \\ \hline \end{array}$$

$0 + 4 = \underline{\quad 4 \quad}$

$$\begin{array}{r} 5 \\ +0 \\ \hline \end{array}$$

$5 + 0 = \underline{\quad 5 \quad}$

$$\begin{array}{r} 0 \\ +5 \\ \hline \end{array}$$

$0 + 5 = \underline{\quad 5 \quad}$

$$\begin{array}{r} 1 \\ +3 \\ \hline \end{array}$$

$1 + 3 = \underline{\quad 4 \quad}$

$$\begin{array}{r} 3 \\ +1 \\ \hline \end{array}$$

$3 + 1 = \underline{\quad 4 \quad}$

MATH

One Step Further

Find four buttons. Find one shirt.
Add how many objects there are.

Sums of 6

Addition

Directions: Add.

$$\begin{array}{r} 1 \\ + 5 \\ \hline 6 \end{array}$$

$$1 + 5 = \underline{\quad 6 \quad}$$

$$\begin{array}{r} 2 \\ + 4 \\ \hline \end{array}$$

$$2 + 4 = \underline{\quad 26 - 26 \quad}$$

$$\begin{array}{r} 5 \\ + 1 \\ \hline 6 \end{array}$$

$$5 + 1 = \underline{\quad 6 \quad}$$

$$\begin{array}{r} 4 \\ + 2 \\ \hline 6 \end{array}$$

$$4 + 2 = \underline{\quad 6 \quad}$$

$$\begin{array}{r} 6 \\ + 0 \\ \hline 6 \end{array}$$

$$6 + 0 = \underline{\quad 6 \quad}$$

$$\begin{array}{r} 3 \\ + 3 \\ \hline 6 \end{array}$$

$$\begin{array}{r} 0 \\ + 6 \\ \hline 6 \end{array}$$

$$0 + 6 = \underline{\quad 6 \quad}$$

$$3 + 3 = \underline{\quad 6 \quad}$$

One Step Further
Color a picture using six different colors.
What colors did you use?

Sums of 7

Directions: Add.

$$\begin{array}{r} 3 \\ +4 \\ \hline 7 \end{array}$$

3 + 4 = ___ 7

$$\begin{array}{r} 6 \\ +1 \\ \hline \end{array}$$

6 + 1 = ___ 7

$$\begin{array}{r} 4 \\ +3 \\ \hline \end{array}$$

4 + 3 = ___ 7

$$\begin{array}{r} 1 \\ +6 \\ \hline \end{array}$$

1 + 6 = ___ 7

$$\begin{array}{r} 7 \\ +0 \\ \hline \end{array}$$

7 + 0 = ___ 7

$$\begin{array}{r} 2 \\ +5 \\ \hline \end{array}$$

2 + 5 = ___ 7

$$\begin{array}{r} 0 \\ +7 \\ \hline \end{array}$$

0 + 7 = ___ 7

$$\begin{array}{r} 5 \\ +2 \\ \hline \end{array}$$

5 + 2 = ___ 7

One Step Further
Roll a die seven times.
What numbers did you roll?

Everyday Success First Grade

MATH

Sums of 8

Directions: Add.

$$\begin{array}{r} 5 \\ +3 \\ \hline 8 \end{array}$$

5 + 3 = _____8_____

$$\begin{array}{r} 7 \\ +1 \\ \hline \end{array}$$

7 + 1 = _____

$$\begin{array}{r} 3 \\ +5 \\ \hline \end{array}$$

3 + 5 = _____

$$\begin{array}{r} 1 \\ +7 \\ \hline \end{array}$$

1 + 7 = _____

$$\begin{array}{r} 2 \\ +6 \\ \hline \end{array}$$

2 + 6 = _____

$$\begin{array}{r} 4 \\ +4 \\ \hline \end{array}$$

$$\begin{array}{r} 6 \\ +2 \\ \hline \end{array}$$

6 + 2 = _____

4 + 4 = _____

One Step Further
Find eight small objects. How many different
piles of two can you separate them into?

Sums of 9

Directions: Add.

$$\begin{array}{r} 2 \\ +7 \\ \hline 9 \end{array}$$

2 + 7 = ___9___

$$\begin{array}{r} 7 \\ +2 \\ \hline \end{array}$$

7 + 2 = ___9___

$$\begin{array}{r} 1 \\ +8 \\ \hline 9 \end{array}$$

1 + 8 = ___9___

$$\begin{array}{r} 8 \\ +1 \\ \hline 9 \end{array}$$

8 + 1 = ___9___

$$\begin{array}{r} 0 \\ +9 \\ \hline 9 \end{array}$$

0 + 9 = ___9___

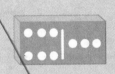

$$\begin{array}{r} 5 \\ +4 \\ \hline 9 \end{array}$$

5 + 4 = ___9___

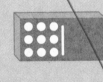

$$\begin{array}{r} 4 \\ +5 \\ \hline 9 \end{array}$$

4 + 5 = ___9___

$$\begin{array}{r} 3 \\ +6 \\ \hline 9 \end{array}$$

3 + 6 = ___9___

$$\begin{array}{r} 6 \\ +3 \\ \hline 9 \end{array}$$

6 + 3 = ___9___

$$\begin{array}{r} 9 \\ +0 \\ \hline 9 \end{array}$$

9 + 0 = ___9___

MATH

One Step Further

Play a game of dominoes with a friend. What is your favorite game to play with friends?

Sums of 10

Addition

Directions: Add.

$$
\begin{array}{r} 7 \\ + \ 3 \\ \hline 10 \end{array}
$$

$7 + 3 = \underline{\quad 10 \quad}$

$$
\begin{array}{r} 3 \\ + \ 7 \\ \hline 10 \end{array}
$$

$3 + 7 = \underline{\quad 10 \quad}$

$1 + 9 = \underline{\quad 10 \quad}$

$2 + 8 = \underline{\quad 10 \quad}$

$$
\begin{array}{r} 1 \\ + \ 9 \\ \hline 10 \end{array}
\qquad
\begin{array}{r} 9 \\ + \ 1 \\ \hline 10 \end{array}
$$

$$
\begin{array}{r} 2 \\ + \ 8 \\ \hline 10 \end{array}
\qquad
\begin{array}{r} 8 \\ + \ 2 \\ \hline 10 \end{array}
$$

$9 + 1 = 10 \quad 10 \quad 10$

$8 + 2 = \underline{\quad 10 \quad}$

$6 + 4 = \underline{\quad 10 \quad}$

$10 + 0 = \underline{\quad 10 \quad}$

$$
\begin{array}{r} 6 \\ + \ 4 \\ \hline 10 \end{array}
\qquad
\begin{array}{r} 4 \\ + \ 6 \\ \hline 10 \end{array}
$$

$$
\begin{array}{r} 10 \\ + \ 0 \\ \hline 10 \end{array}
\qquad
\begin{array}{r} 0 \\ +10 \\ \hline 10 \end{array}
$$

$4 + 6 = \underline{\quad 10 \quad}$

$0 + 10 = \underline{\quad 10 \quad}$

One Step Further
Find your favorite book. Read the first 10 lines out loud.

Addition 1, 2

Directions: Count the cats and tell how many.

_2_

_3_

_4_

MATH

One Step Further
Add the number of cats you have to the number of cats your friend has.

Addition 3, 4, 5, 6

Directions: Practice writing the numbers and then add. Draw dots to help, if needed.

3   3

4   4

5   5

6   6

$$2 \atop +4 \over 6$$ $$1 \atop +4 \over 5$$

$$3 \atop +2 \over 5$$ $$1 \atop +2 \over 3$$

One Step Further
Count the pillows on your bed. Then, count the blankets. Add them together.

Addition 7, 8, 9

Directions: Practice writing the numbers and then add. Draw dots to help, if needed.

7   7

8   9

9   4

$$8 + 1 = 9$$

$$3 + 5 = 8$$

$$2 + 7 = 9$$

$$6 + 1 = 7$$

1 2 3 4 5 6 7 8 9

One Step Further
Divide your crayons into two piles. Count the crayons and add each group together.

Addition

The Barton family is having a picnic. But the ants have carried away their food.

Directions: Use an addition equation to find out how many ants took food. The first one is done for you.

How many ants carried away fruit?

$$\underline{1} + \underline{2} = \underline{3}$$

How many ants carried away vegetables?

$$\underline{2} + \underline{3} = \underline{5}$$

How many ants carried away hot dogs?

$$\underline{3} + \underline{3} = \underline{6}$$

How many ants carried away bread?

$$\underline{5} + \underline{2} = \underline{7}$$

One Step Further
Have a picnic with your family.
What foods do you eat?

Addition

Directions: Add up the dots on the domino pieces below. Write the total on the line below each piece.

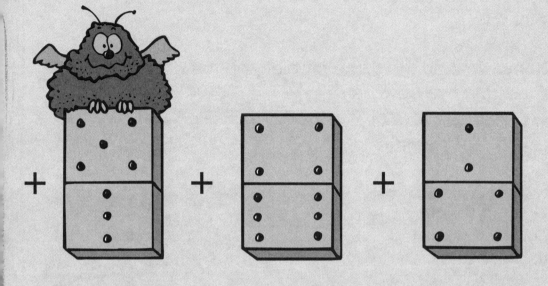

+ _____   + _____   + _____

Directions: Now, draw the missing dots on each domino. Make sure the total number of dots adds up to the total on the line below each domino.

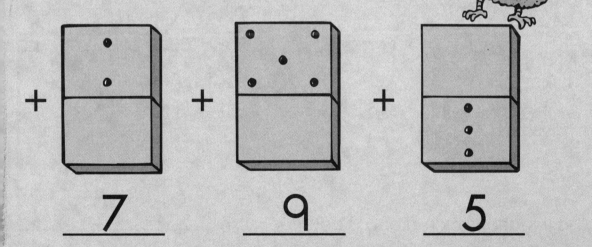

+ 7   + 9   + 5

One Step Further
Find some dominoes.
Add up the dots on each domino.

Addition

Mrs. Murky asked three monster girls and two monster boys to come to the front of the class. She said, "If I have three monster girls and I add two monster boys, how many monster children do I have all together?"

Directions: Now, do the same problem on the board, but count the two boys first.

$$3 + 2 = \underline{5}$$

$$2 + \underline{3} = \underline{5}$$

Does it matter which group is counted first? _____

One Step Further

How many girls are in your class at school?
How many boys?

Problem Solving

Directions: Solve each problem.

There are five white .

There are four blue  .

How many in all?

$$\begin{array}{r} 5 \\ +4 \\ \hline \end{array}$$

There are three  .

Seven more come.

How many are there now?

Beth has nine .

She buys one more.

Now how many does she have?

There are six .

There are three .

How many in all?

There were eight .

Two more came.

Then how many were there?

One Step Further
How many T-shirts do you own? How many
would you own if you bought one more?

Everyday Success First Grade

Plenty to Wear!

Directions: The key words "in all" tell you to add. Circle the key words "in all" and solve the problems.

1. Jack has four white shirts and two yellow shirts. How many shirts does Jack have in all?

$$4 \bigcirc 2 = \text{\_\_\_\_}$$

2. Allison has four pink blouses and six red ones. How many blouses does Allison have in all?

$$4 \bigcirc 6 = \text{\_\_\_\_}$$

4. Charley has three pairs of summer pants and eight pairs of winter pants. How many pairs of pants does Charley have in all?

$$3 \bigcirc 8 = \text{\_\_\_\_}$$

3. Betsy has two black skirts and seven blue skirts. In all, how many skirts does Betsy have?

$$2 \bigcirc 7 = \text{\_\_\_\_}$$

5. Jeff has five knit hats and five cloth hats. How many hats does Jeff have in all?

$$5 \bigcirc 5 = \text{\_\_\_\_}$$

One Step Further
How many shoes do you own?
How many are winter shoes?

Problems in the Park

Directions: Circle the addition key words "in all." Write a number sentence to solve each problem.

1. At the park, there are three baseball games and six basketball games being played. How many games are being played in all?

_____

2. In the park, nine mothers are pushing their babies in strollers and eight are carrying their babies in baskets. How many mothers in all have their babies with them in the park?

_____

3. On one team, there are five boys and three girls. How many team members are there in all?

_____

4. At one time, there were eight men and four boys pitching horseshoes. In all, how many people were pitching horseshoes?

_____

5. While playing basketball, four of the players were wearing gym shoes and six were not. How many basketball players were there in all?

_____

MATH

One Step Further
Think of a team you have been on.
How many people were on the team?

Additional Story Problems

Directions: Circle the addition key words "in all." Write a number sentence to solve each problem.

1. On the block where Cindy lives, there are seven brick houses and five stone houses. How many houses are there in all?

_____

2. One block from Cindy's house, there are six white houses and four gray houses. How many houses are there in all?

_____

3. Children live in eight of the two-story houses and two of the one-story houses. How many houses in all have children living in them?

_____

4. Near Cindy's house, there are three grocery stores and five discount stores. How many stores are there in all?

_____

5. In Cindy's neighborhood, four students are in high school and nine are in elementary school. In all, how many children are in school?

_____

One Step Further
Count the number of houses on the street you live on.

Solving Stories

Directions: Write a number sentence to solve each problem.

1. Brad ate five slices of pizza. Todd ate three. How many slices of pizza did both boys eat? _____

2. Sam scored four points for the team. Dave scored four points. How many points did Sam and Dave score? _____

3. Missy bought six dresses. Dot bought three. How many dresses did they buy in all? _____

4. Once there were three bears having a picnic. Then, two more bears joined the fun. Now, how many bears were having a picnic? _____

MATH

One Step Further
What is your favorite kind of pizza?
How many slices do you like to eat?

Everyday Success First Grade

MATH

Beary Good

Directions: Put counters on each bear to add. Write the sums below.

$$\begin{array}{r} 6 \\ +1 \\ \hline 7 \end{array} \qquad \begin{array}{r} 3 \\ +4 \\ \hline 7 \end{array} \qquad \begin{array}{r} 2 \\ +3 \\ \hline 5 \end{array} \qquad \begin{array}{r} 5 \\ +2 \\ \hline 7 \end{array} \qquad \begin{array}{r} 7 \\ +1 \\ \hline 8 \end{array}$$

$$\begin{array}{r} 8 \\ +0 \\ \hline 8 \end{array} \qquad \begin{array}{r} 4 \\ +5 \\ \hline 9 \end{array} \qquad \begin{array}{r} 3 \\ +6 \\ \hline 9 \end{array} \qquad \begin{array}{r} 2 \\ +6 \\ \hline 8 \end{array} \qquad \begin{array}{r} 3 \\ +5 \\ \hline 8 \end{array}$$

One Step Further

How many teddy bears do you own?
Are teddy bears your favorite toy?

Air Bear Addition

Directions: Help Buddy off the ground. Add to find the sum. Then, color the clouds with sums of 9 to find the right path.

$5 + 5 = 10$

$7 + 4 = 11$

$3 + 7 = 10$

$6 + 3 = 9$

$8 + 1 = 9$

$6 + 4 = 10$

$2 + 7 = 9$

$2 + 5 = 7$

$5 + 4 = 9$

$10 + 1 = 11$

$6 + 5 = 11$

$3 + 4 = 7$

$9 + 0 = 9$

$2 + 5 = 7$

$2 + 4 = 6$

$5 + 5 = 10$

$4 + 5 = 6$

$3 + 2 = 5$

$2 + 6 = 8$

$8 + 2 = 10$

$3 + 6 = 9$

One Step Further
Look up in the sky. How many clouds can you see?

Practicing Addition

Addition Practice

Directions: Add.

6 +4 ___ 10	7 +2 ___ 9	4 +4 ___ 8	4 +5 ___ 9	9 +1 ___
2 +7 ___ 9	6 +2 ___ 8	9 +0 ___ 9	2 +5 ___ 7	1 +4 ___ 5
8 +1 ___ 9	2 +2 ___ 4	3 +6 ___ 9	1 +7 ___ 8	7 +3 ___ 10
2 +3 ___ 5	2 +8 ___ 10	3 +5 ___ 8	8 +2 ___ 10	6 +1 ___ 7
1 +9 ___ 10	6 +3 ___ 9	3 +4 ___ 7	5 +2 ___ 7	5 +4 ___ 8

One Step Further
What two numbers add up to equal
your age?

Counting Kittens

Subtraction means "taking away" or subtracting one number from another. The symbol for subtraction is called a **minus sign (−)**. It means to subtract the second number from the first.

Directions: Use counters to subtract. Make a group, then take some away. Write how many are left.

_____
are left

Put in 4. Take away 1.

_____
are left

Put in 5. Take away 2.

_____
are left

Put in 7. Take away 3.

One Step Further
Tell a story about three kittens.
Don't forget to give the kittens names.

What's the Difference?

Directions: Use counters to subtract.

Put in 5. Take away 2.

How many counters are left? ___3___

The number that tells how many are left is called the **difference**.
The difference of 5 – 2 is 3.

Directions: Use counters to find each difference.

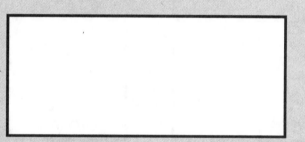

6 – 3 = _____

5 – 1 = _____

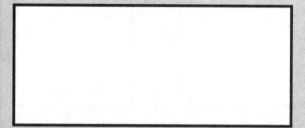

5 – 3 = _____

4 – 2 = _____

One Step Further
Name a place you might see a clown.
What does a clown do?

Subtracting from 1, 2, and 3

Directions: Subtract.

$$\begin{array}{r} 3 \\ -1 \\ \hline 2 \end{array}$$

$$3 - 1 = \underline{\quad 2 \quad}$$

$$\begin{array}{r} 2 \\ -1 \\ \hline 1 \end{array}$$

$$2 - 1 = \underline{\quad 1 \quad}$$

$$\begin{array}{r} 3 \\ -2 \\ \hline 1 \end{array}$$

$$3 - 2 = \underline{\quad 1 \quad}$$

$$\begin{array}{r} 1 \\ -0 \\ \hline 1 \end{array}$$

$$1 - 0 = \underline{\quad 1 \quad}$$

$$\begin{array}{r} 3 \\ -0 \\ \hline 3 \end{array}$$

$$3 - 0 = \underline{\quad 3 \quad}$$

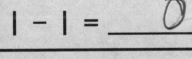

$$\begin{array}{r} 1 \\ -1 \\ \hline 0 \end{array}$$

$$1 - 1 = \underline{\quad 0 \quad}$$

$$\begin{array}{r} 2 \\ -2 \\ \hline 0 \end{array}$$

$$2 - 2 = \underline{\quad 0 \quad}$$

$$\begin{array}{r} 3 \\ -3 \\ \hline 0 \end{array}$$

$$3 - 3 = \underline{\quad 0 \quad}$$

One Step Further
How many birds can you see out
your window?

Everyday Success First Grade

Subtracting from 4 and 5

Directions: Subtract.

$$\begin{array}{r} 5 \\ -1 \\ \hline 4 \end{array}$$

$$\begin{array}{r} 4 \\ -3 \\ \hline \end{array}$$

5 - 1 = __4__

4 - 3 = __1__

$$\begin{array}{r} 5 \\ -4 \\ \hline 1 \end{array}$$

$$\begin{array}{r} 4 \\ -4 \\ \hline 0 \end{array}$$

5 - 4 = __1__

4 - 4 = __0__

$$\begin{array}{r} 5 \\ -2 \\ \hline 3 \end{array}$$

$$\begin{array}{r} 4 \\ -2 \\ \hline 2 \end{array}$$

5 - 2 = __3__

4 - 2 = __2__

One Step Further

Set up five blocks. Knock two of them over.
How many are left standing?

Subtracting from 6

Directions: Subtract.

$$\begin{array}{r} 6 \\ -1 \\ \hline 5 \end{array}$$

$6 - 1 = \underline{\quad 5 \quad}$

$$\begin{array}{r} 6 \\ -5 \\ \hline 1 \end{array}$$

$6 - 5 = \underline{\quad 1 \quad}$

$$\begin{array}{r} 6 \\ -4 \\ \hline 2 \end{array}$$

$6 - 4 = \underline{\quad 2 \quad}$

$$\begin{array}{r} 6 \\ -2 \\ \hline 4 \end{array}$$

$6 - 2 = \underline{\quad 4 \quad}$

$$\begin{array}{r} 6 \\ -3 \\ \hline 3 \end{array}$$

$6 - 3 = \underline{\quad 3 \quad}$

$$\begin{array}{r} 6 \\ -0 \\ \hline 6 \end{array}$$

$6 - 0 = \underline{\quad 6 \quad}$

MATH

One Step Further
Draw six flowers for the bees to land on.
Color each flower a different color.

Subtracting from 7

Directions: Subtract.

$$
\begin{array}{r}
7 \\
-6 \\
\hline 1
\end{array}
$$

$7 - 6 =$ **1**

$$
\begin{array}{r}
7 \\
-1 \\
\hline
\end{array}
$$

$7 - 1 =$ **6**

$$
\begin{array}{r}
7 \\
-3 \\
\hline 9
\end{array}
$$

$7 - 3 =$ **4**

$$
\begin{array}{r}
7 \\
-4 \\
\hline 3
\end{array}
$$

$7 - 4 =$ **3**

$$
\begin{array}{r}
7 \\
-7 \\
\hline 0
\end{array}
$$

$7 - 7 =$ **0**

$$
\begin{array}{r}
7 \\
-0 \\
\hline 7
\end{array}
$$

$7 - 0 =$ **7**

$$
\begin{array}{r}
7 \\
-2 \\
\hline 5
\end{array}
$$

$7 - 2 =$ **5**

$$
\begin{array}{r}
7 \\
-5 \\
\hline 2
\end{array}
$$

$7 - 5 =$ **2**

One Step Further
Name the seven days of the week.
What day is your favorite?

Subtracting from 8

Directions: Subtract.

$$\begin{array}{r} 8 \\ -7 \\ \hline 1 \end{array}$$

$8 - 7 =$ __1__

$$\begin{array}{r} 8 \\ -1 \\ \hline 7 \end{array}$$

$8 - 1 =$ __7__

$$\begin{array}{r} 8 \\ -2 \\ \hline 6 \end{array}$$

$8 - 2 =$ __6__

$$\begin{array}{r} 8 \\ -6 \\ \hline 2 \end{array}$$

$8 - 6 =$ __2__

$$\begin{array}{r} 8 \\ -4 \\ \hline 4 \end{array}$$

$8 - 4 =$ __4__

$$\begin{array}{r} 8 \\ -8 \\ \hline 0 \end{array}$$

$8 - 8 =$ __0__

$$\begin{array}{r} 8 \\ -3 \\ \hline 5 \end{array}$$

$8 - 3 =$ __5__

$$\begin{array}{r} 8 \\ -5 \\ \hline 3 \end{array}$$

$8 - 5 =$ __3__

One Step Further
Can you name at least eight states?
What state do you live in?

Everyday Success First Grade

Subtracting from 9

Subtraction

Directions: Subtract.

$$\begin{array}{r} 9 \\ -6 \\ \hline 3 \end{array}$$

$9 - 6 =$ ___3___

$$\begin{array}{r} 9 \\ -3 \\ \hline \end{array}$$

$9 - 3 =$ ___6___

$$\begin{array}{r} 9 \\ -0 \\ \hline \end{array}$$

$9 - 0 =$ ___9___

$$\begin{array}{r} 9 \\ -9 \\ \hline \end{array}$$

$9 - 9 =$ ___0___

$$\begin{array}{r} 9 \\ -5 \\ \hline \end{array}$$

$9 - 5 =$ ___4___

$$\begin{array}{r} 9 \\ -4 \\ \hline \end{array}$$

$9 - 4 =$ ___5___

$$\begin{array}{r} 9 \\ -8 \\ \hline \end{array}$$

$9 - 8 =$ ___1___

$$\begin{array}{r} 9 \\ -1 \\ \hline \end{array}$$

$9 - 1 =$ ___8___

One Step Further
Roll two dice. How many rolls do you make
until you roll a total of nine?

Subtracting from 10

Directions: Subtract.

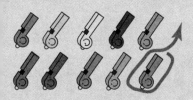

$$\begin{array}{r} 10 \\ -\ 1 \\ \hline 9 \end{array}$$

$10 - 1 = \underline{\quad 9 \quad}$

$$\begin{array}{r} 10 \\ -\ 9 \\ \hline 1 \end{array}$$

$10 - 9 = \underline{\quad 1 \quad}$

$10 - 7 = \underline{\quad 3 \quad}$

$$\begin{array}{r} 10 \\ -\ 7 \\ \hline 3 \end{array} \qquad \begin{array}{r} 10 \\ -\ 3 \\ \hline 7 \end{array}$$

$10 - 3 = \underline{\quad 7 \quad}$

$10 - 4 = \underline{\quad 6 \quad}$

$$\begin{array}{r} 10 \\ -\ 4 \\ \hline 6 \end{array} \qquad \begin{array}{r} 10 \\ -\ 6 \\ \hline 4 \end{array}$$

$10 - 6 = \underline{\quad 4 \quad}$

$10 - 8 = \underline{\quad 2 \quad}$

$$\begin{array}{r} 10 \\ -\ 8 \\ \hline 2 \end{array} \qquad \begin{array}{r} 10 \\ -\ 2 \\ \hline 8 \end{array}$$

$10 - 2 = \underline{\quad 8 \quad}$

$$\begin{array}{r} 10 \\ -\ 0 \\ \hline 10 \end{array}$$

$10 - 0 = \underline{\quad 10 \quad}$

MATH

One Step Further
Can you whistle? Try to whistle for 10 seconds while standing on one foot.

Everyday Success First Grade

Subtraction 1, 2, 3

Directions: Practice writing the numbers and then subtract. Draw dots and cross them out, if needed.

MATH

$$
\begin{array}{r} 3 \\ -1 \\ \hline \end{array}
\qquad
\begin{array}{r} 4 \\ -3 \\ \hline \end{array}
$$

$$
\begin{array}{r} 2 \\ -1 \\ \hline \end{array}
\qquad
\begin{array}{r} 3 \\ -2 \\ \hline \end{array}
$$

One Step Further

Ask an adult for a plate of three carrots.
Eat one. How many carrots are left?

Subtraction 4, 5, 6

Directions: Practice writing the numbers and then subtract. Draw dots and cross them out, if needed.

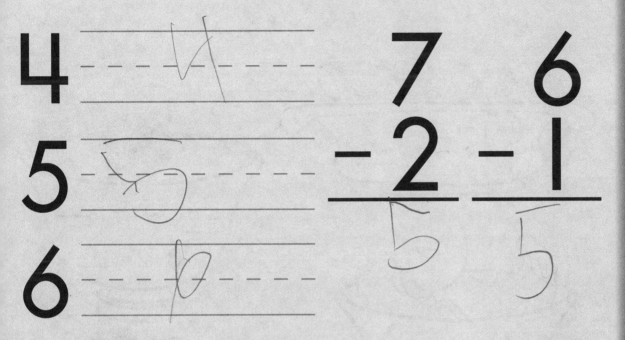

4

5

6

$$7 - 2 = 5$$

$$6 - 1 = 5$$

$$6 - 2 = 4$$

$$5 - 1 = 4$$

MATH

One Step Further
Fill five cups with water. Dump out two cups. How many cups still have water in them?

Everyday Success First Grade

Nutty Subtraction

Directions: Count the nuts in each dish. Write the answer on the line by each dish. Circle each problem with the same answer.

3

4 - 1 = ___

= ___

5 - 2 = ___

2
−2

5
−2

5 - 4 = ___

3 - 2 = ___

4 - 0 = ___

5 - 1 = ___

2
−2

5 - 0 = ___

5   2
−1   −2

4   5
−1   −3

4 - 2 = ___

One Step Further
Find five peanuts or other small objects.
Take away two. How many are left?

Subtracting

Six silly green frogs were sitting on six lily pads.

A big bird flew by and two frogs jumped off into the water.

Directions: Solve the subtraction problem by answering the questions.

How many frogs were sitting on the lily pads? _____

How many frogs jumped off? _____

How many frogs were left? _____

One Step Further

Hop like a frog four times. How many birds can you see outside right now?

Everyday Success First Grade

MATH

Subtracting

Four hungry cats went
on a picnic.

Two cats spotted some mice
and took off to catch them!

Directions: Solve the subtraction problem by answering
the questions.

How many cats went on the picnic? _____

How many cats ran after the mice? _____

How many cats were left? _____

One Step Further
Tell a story about the cats' picnic.
What happened before the mice came?

How Many Animals Are Left?

Directions: The key word "left" tells you to subtract. Circle the key word "left." Write a number sentence to solve each subtraction problem.

1. Bill had 10 kittens, but four of them ran away. How many kittens does he have left?

$$10 - 4 = 6$$
_____

2. There were 12 rabbits eating in the garden. Dogs chased three of them away. How many rabbits were left?

_____

3. There were 14 frogs on the bank of the pond. Then, nine of them hopped into the water. How many frogs were left on the bank?

_____

4. Bill saw 11 birds eating from the bird feeders in his backyard. A cat scared seven of them away. How many birds were left at the feeders?

_____

5. Bill counted 15 robins in his yard. Then, eight of the robins flew away. How many robins were left in the yard?

_____

MATH

One Step Further

Is there a bird feeder in your yard?
How many birds are eating from the feeder?

How Many Left?

Directions: Solve each problem.

There are 10 white .

There are four blue .

How many more white than blue are there? _____ 6

$$\begin{array}{r} 10 \\ -\ 4 \\ \hline 6 \end{array}$$

Ten are on the table.

Two are broken.

How many are not broken? _____ 8

There are nine .

Six swim away.

How many are left? _____ 3

Joni wants nine .

She has five .

How many more does she need? _____ 4

There were 10 .

Five melted.

How many did not melt? _____ 5

One Step Further
What color flowers are outside your home?
Draw a picture of your favorite flower.

Subtraction

Directions: Solve the problems.

Once there was a monster named Miles, who spent every day playing marbles. He kept his 20 favorite marbles in a beautiful marble bag. One day, he grabbed his marbles and went to play with his friends.

At Wilbur's house, he lost 10 marbles. How many marbles did he have left?

Fill in the blank and carry down the total to the next blank.

$20 - 10 = \underline{\hspace{1cm}}$

At Rosie's house, he lost two more! Carry down the total to the next blank.

$\underline{\hspace{1cm}} - 2 = \underline{\hspace{1cm}}$

At Fuddy's house, he lost three more!

$\underline{\hspace{1cm}} - 3 = \underline{\hspace{1cm}}$

At Matilda's house, he lost four more!

$\underline{\hspace{1cm}} - 4 = \underline{\hspace{1cm}}$

What a sad day for Miles! How many marbles did he have left? _____

MATH

One Step Further
How many marbles do you own?
Do you have more or fewer than Miles?

Subtracting

You and Oliver Opossum have **25¢** to buy some of these toys.

Directions: When you buy a toy, cross it out. Then, write the cost in the table. The first toy is crossed out for you. Each time you buy a toy, subtract it until you have **no more money** to spend.

25 ¢	–	4 ¢	=	21 ¢
21 ¢	–	___ ¢	=	___ ¢
___ ¢	–	___ ¢	=	___ ¢
___ ¢	–	___ ¢	=	___ ¢
___ ¢	–	___ ¢	=	___ ¢
___ ¢	–	___ ¢	=	___ ¢

One Step Further
What toy would you most like to buy for a friend?

Picture Problems

Directions: Solve the number problem under each picture. Write **+** or **–** to show if you should add or subtract.

How many  in all?

$7 \quad 5 =$ _____

How many s are left?

$8 \quad 3 =$ _____

How many s are left?

$9 \quad 4 =$ _____

How many s in all?

$14 \quad 1 =$ _____

How many ✏s are left?

$15 \quad 6 =$ _____

How many 🧶s in all?

$9 \quad 5 =$ _____

One Step Further
Grab some pencils. Take away three of them.
How many are left?

MATH

Everyday Success First Grade

Puppy Problems

Directions: Look at the pictures. Complete the number sentences.

5 ◯ 6 = _____   11 ◯ 4 = _____

12 ◯ 7 = _____   7 ◯ 6 = _____

5 ◯ 5 = _____   8 ◯ 6 = _____

One Step Further
Name your favorite book or movie
about dogs.

It's Show Time!

Directions: It's time for Ellie and Elmer to perform! Look at the problems below. Write **+** or **−** to complete each number sentence. Then, connect all the **+** peanuts to lead Ellie to her stool. Connect all the **−** peanuts to connect Elmer to his stool.

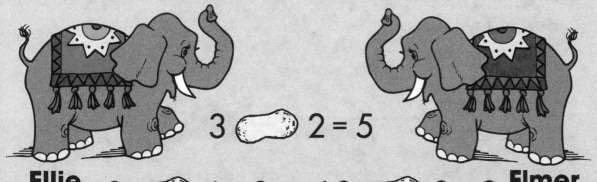

Ellie   **Elmer**

$3 \bigcirc 2 = 5$

$2 \bigcirc 6 = 8$ $10 \bigcirc 8 = 2$

$8 \bigcirc 2 = 6$ $5 \bigcirc 4 = 9$ $7 \bigcirc 3 = 4$

$9 \bigcirc 4 = 5$ $10 \bigcirc 3 = 7$ $5 \bigcirc 5 = 10$

$3 \bigcirc 3 = 0$ $9 \bigcirc 1 = 10$ $7 \bigcirc 5 = 2$

$6 \bigcirc 3 = 3$ $6 \bigcirc 4 = 10$ $5 \bigcirc 2 = 7$

$5 \bigcirc 3 = 8$

$2 \bigcirc 7 = 9$

One Step Further
Tell a story about a day at the circus.
What do you like most about the circus?

Everyday Success First Grade

Add or Subtract?

Directions: The key words "in all" tell you to add. The key word "left" tells you to subtract. Circle the key words and write **+** or **−** in the circles. Then, solve the problems.

1. The pet store has three large dogs and five small dogs. How many dogs are there in all?

$$3 \; \bigoplus \; 5 = \text{_____}$$

2. The pet store had nine parrots and then sold four of them. How many parrots does the pet store have left?

$$9 \; \bigcirc \; 4 = \text{_____}$$

3. At the pet store, three of the eight kittens were sold. How many kittens are left in the pet store?

$$8 \; \bigcirc \; 3 = \text{_____}$$

4. The pet store gave Linda's class two adult gerbils and nine young ones. How many gerbils did Linda's class get in all?

$$2 \; \bigcirc \; 9 = \text{_____}$$

5. The monkey at the pet store has five rubber toys and four wooden toys. How many toys does the monkey have in all?

$$5 \; \bigcirc \; 4 = \text{_____}$$

One Step Further
What pet would you most like to have from a pet store?

Addition and Subtraction

Directions: Solve the problems.

$1 + 3 =$ ___ 2

$4 - 3 =$ ___ 1

$4 + 5 =$ ___ 9

$6 + 1 =$ ___ 7

$7 - 2 =$ ___ 5

$8 - 4 =$ ___ 4

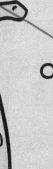

$9 - 1 =$ ___ 8

$10 - 3 =$ ___ 7

$5 - 2 =$ ___ 3

$6 + 3 =$ ___ 9

$8 + 2 =$ ___ 6

$5 + 5 =$ ___ 10

MATH

One Step Further
What is your favorite zoo animal?
What do you like about it?

Everyday Success First Grade

Addition and Subtraction

Remember, addition means "putting together" or adding two or more numbers to find the sum. Subtraction means "taking away" or subtracting one number from another.

Review

Directions: Solve the problems. From your answers, use the code to color the quilt.

Color:

6 = **blue**
7 = yellow
8 = **green**
9 = **red**
10 = orange

MATH

One Step Further
What color quilt or blanket do you have on your bed?

Whole and Half

A **fraction** is a number that names part of a whole, such as ½ or ¾.

Directions: Color half of each object.

Example:

Whole apple   **Half an apple** $\dfrac{1}{2}$

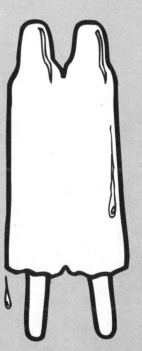

MATH

Thirds

Directions: Circle the objects that have three equal parts.

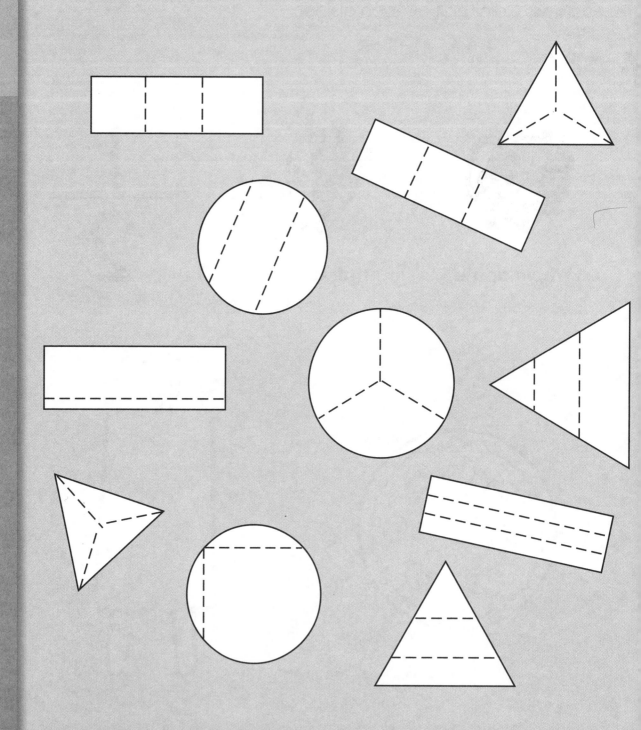

One Step Further
What's for dinner tonight?
Divide your food into three equal parts.

Fourths

Directions: Circle the objects that have four equal parts.

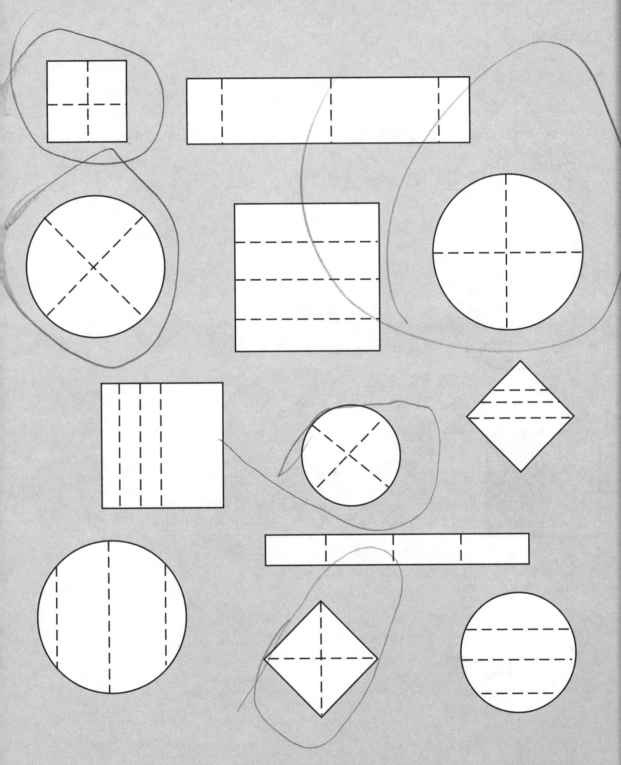

MATH

One Step Further
Ask an adult to cut an apple into four equal parts.

Review

Fractions

Directions: Count the equal parts. Then, write the fraction.

Example:

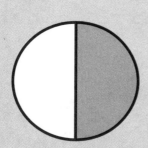

Shaded part = ___1___   Write

Equal parts = ___3___ $\frac{1}{3}$

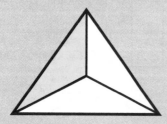

Shaded part = _____   Write

Equal parts = _____   ___

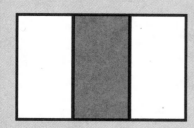

Shaded part = _____   Write

Equal parts = _____   ___

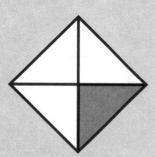

Shaded part = _____   Write

Equal parts = _____   ___

One Step Further

Split a banana into two parts. Then, split the parts again. How many parts are there?

Fractions

One day, the monsters went to the pizza stand for a snack.

- Mug ate $\frac{1}{2}$ of a pizza.

- Lug ate $\frac{2}{4}$ of a pizza.

- Gug ate $\frac{3}{6}$ of a pizza.

Directions: Color the portion of pizza that each monster ate.

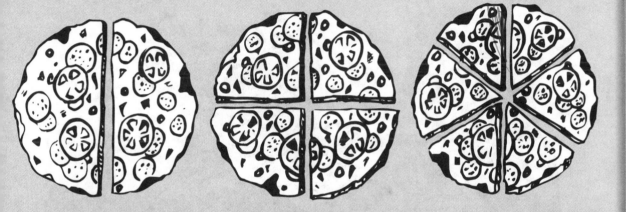

Which monster ate the most pizza?_____

Explain your answer.

_____

_____

_____

One Step Further
What toppings do you like on your pizza?
Do you eat as much as Mug, Lug, or Gug?

Everyday Success First Grade

Fractions

Suji and Samantha had Millie and Milo over to play after school. Their mother gave them a plate of cookies to share. If they divide the cookies equally, how many cookies will there be for each monster?

Directions: Draw the cookies on the plates to show how many each monster gets.

One Step Further
What do you like to eat for an after-school snack?

Fractions

The monsters are getting in shape.

Directions: Look below and on page 138 to see the different ways they are working out. Then, answer the questions on page 138.

One Step Further
What is your favorite way to get in shape?
Do you exercise with a friend?

Fractions

Directions: Answer the questions and fill in the blanks below. The first one is done for you.

How many monsters touch their toes?

___1___ out of 10 monsters, or ___1___ of the monsters.
___10___

How many monsters hang upside down?

_____ out of 10 monsters, or _____ of the monsters.
___10___

How many of the monsters ride the bikes?

_____ out of 10 monsters, or _____ of the monsters.
___10___

How many of the monsters run on the treadmill?

_____ out of 10 monsters, or _____ of the monsters.
___10___

How many monsters lift weights?

_____ out of 10 monsters, or _____ of the monsters.
___10___

How many monsters do leg lifts?

_____ out of 10 monsters, or _____ of the monsters.
___10___

One Step Further
Touch your toes five times. Then, go outside and ride your bike with a friend.

Inch

An **inch** is a unit of length.

Directions: Cut off the ruler. How long is each object?

_____ inches

_____ inches

_____ inches

_____ inches

_____ inches

_____ inches

_____ inch

8
7
6
5
4
3
2
1

inches

MATH

One Step Further
Measure the pencil you are using to
complete this book. How long is it?

This page is blank for cutting exercise on previous page.

Inch

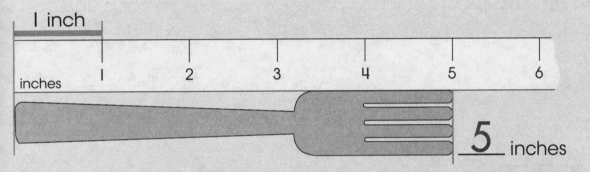

Directions: How long is each object?

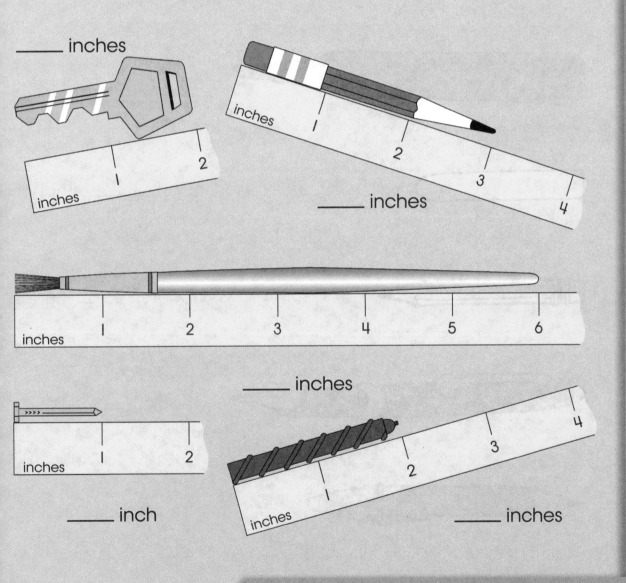

_____ inches

_____ inches

_____ inches

_____ inch

_____ inches

One Step Further
Find something in your home that is only one inch long.

Inch by Inch

Directions: Use the ruler on page 139 to measure each object below to the nearest inch.

 about _____ inch

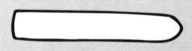 about _____ inch

 about _____ inches

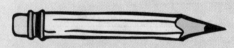 about _____ inches

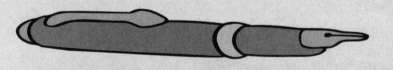 about _____ inches

 about _____ inches

about _____ inches

One Step Further
Measure a carrot. Is it longer or shorter than the objects on this page?

"Reel" 'Em In!

Directions: Use the ruler on page 139 to measure the fish to the nearest inch.

about _____ inches

about _____ inch

about _____ inch

about _____ inches

about _____ inches

about _____ inches

One Step Further
Which fish on this page would you like to have? Why?

Everyday Success First Grade

The Inch Worm

Directions: Use the ruler on page 139 to measure these worms to the nearest inch.

1. _____   2. _____

3. _____

4. _____   5. _____

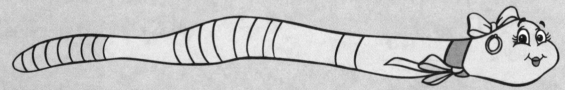

6. _____

7. _____

One Step Further
Draw a picture of a worm that is longer than
all the worms on this page.

Centimeter

A **centimeter** is a unit of length.

Directions: Cut off the ruler. How long is each object?

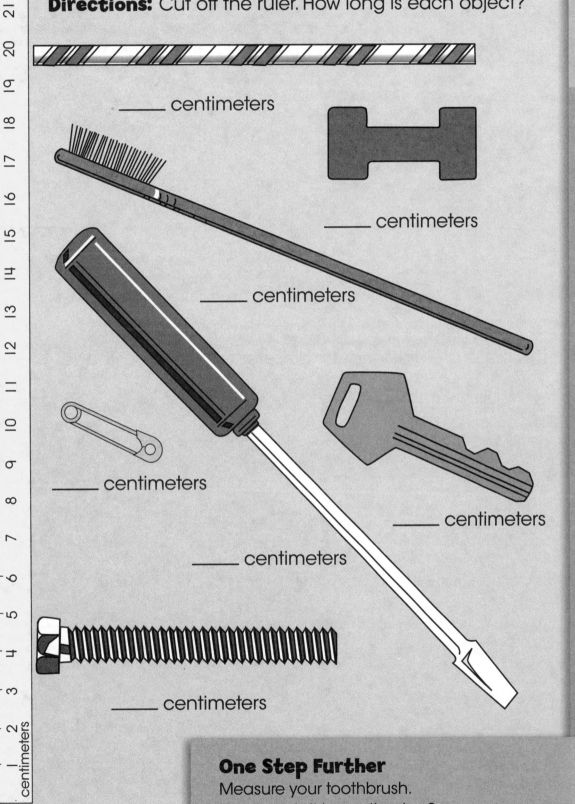

_____ centimeters

_____ centimeters

_____ centimeters

_____ centimeters

_____ centimeters

_____ centimeters

_____ centimeters

One Step Further
Measure your toothbrush.
How long is it in centimeters?

This page is blank for cutting exercise on previous page.

Centimeter

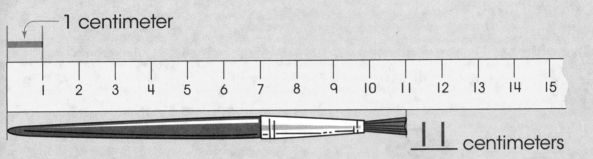

1 centimeter

| 1 | 2 | 3 | 4 | 5 | 6 | 7 | 8 | 9 | 10 | 11 | 12 | 13 | 14 | 15 |

_____ centimeters

Directions: How long is each object?

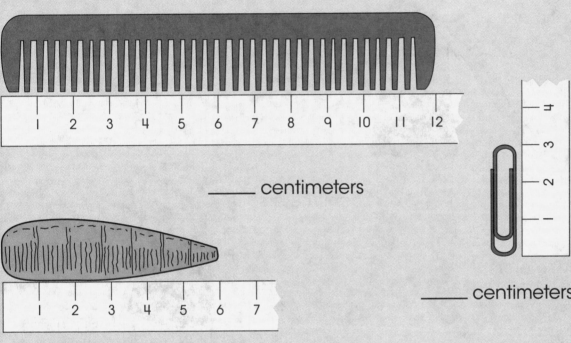

_____ centimeters

_____ centimeters

_____ centimeters

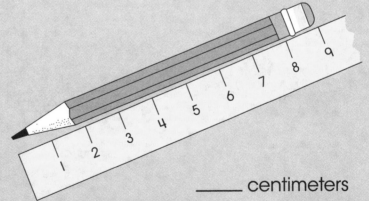

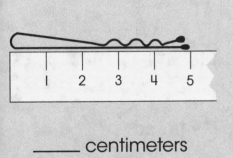

_____ centimeters

_____ centimeters

One Step Further
Go back to the object you found that was
one inch long. How many centimeters is it?

MATH

Measuring

Work with a friend.

Directions: Use the centimeter ruler on page 145. Measure each other.

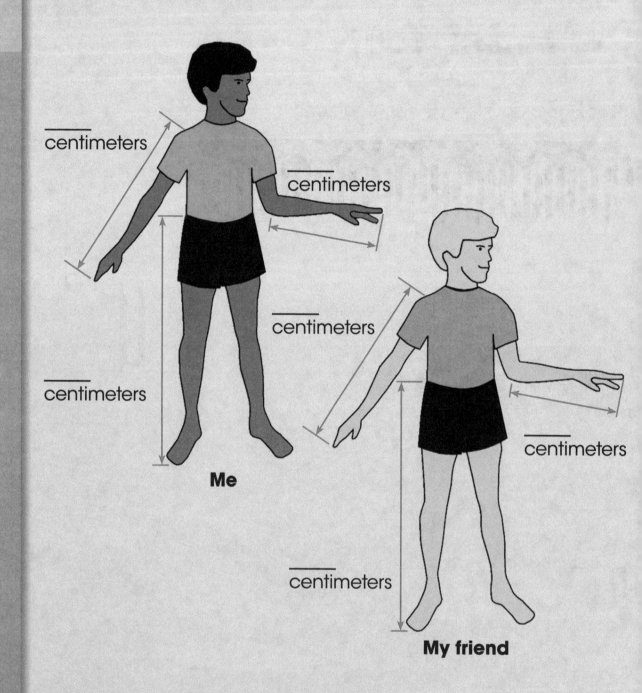

_____ centimeters

_____ centimeters

_____ centimeters

_____ centimeters

Me

_____ centimeters

_____ centimeters

_____ centimeters

My friend

One Step Further
With a friend, measure your hand to the nearest centimeter. Then, measure your foot.

Brush Up on Measuring!

Directions: Use the centimeter ruler on page 145 to measure
these brushes to the nearest centimeter.

about _____ centimeters

about _____ centimeters

about _____ centimeters

about _____ centimeters

about _____ centimeters

about _____ centimeters

about _____ centimeters

about _____ centimeters

about _____ centimeters

One Step Further
Paint a picture of your favorite day.
What did you paint?

Everyday Success First Grade

Flowers That "Measure" Up

Directions: Use the centimeter ruler on page 145 to measure how tall each flower is. Measure each flower from the bottom of the stem to the top of the flower. Write the answer on the blank by the flower.

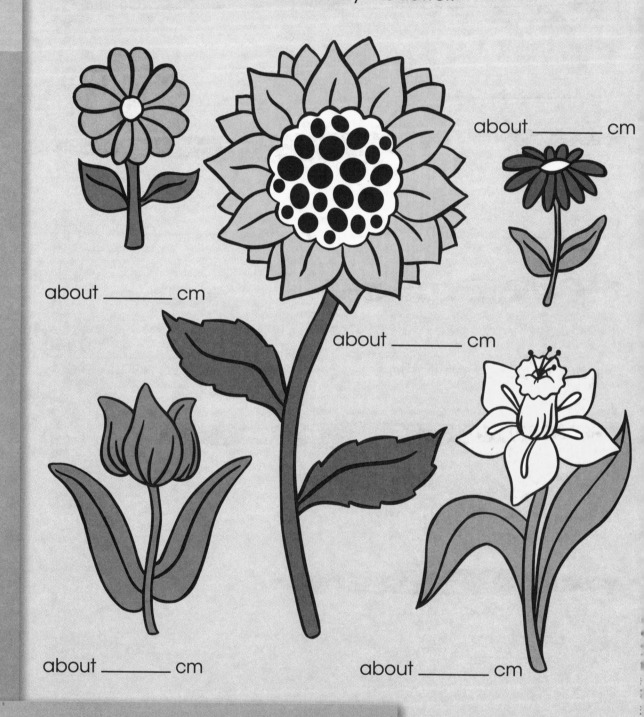

about _____ cm

about _____ cm

about _____ cm

about _____ cm

about _____ cm

One Step Further

Find a flower in your neighborhood.
Measure it to the nearest centimeter.

How Far Is It?

Directions: Use the inch ruler on page 139 to measure each distance on the map. Then, use the letters on the circles and your answers to solve the message at the bottom of the page.

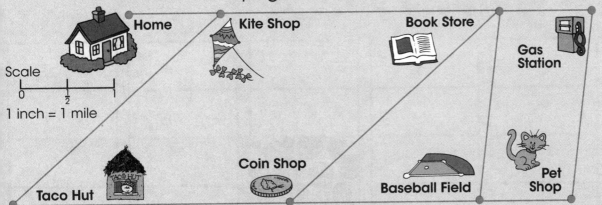

Scale
1 inch = 1 mile

How far is it from . . .

1. home to the Kite Shop? _____ (s)

2. the Kite Shop to the Book Store to the
   Coin Shop? _____ (e)

3. home to the Kite Shop to the Taco Hut? _____ (p)

4. the Taco Hut to the Coin Shop to the
   Book Store to the Gas Station? _____ (a)

5. the Taco Hut to the Coin Shop? _____ (u)

6. the Baseball Field to the Book Store to
   the Kite Shop? _____ (d)

7. the Pet Shop to the Gas Station? _____ (r)

8. the Gas Station to the Pet Shop to the Baseball
   Field to the Coin Shop to the Taco Hut? _____ (m)

MATH

You ___ ___ ___ ___ ___ ___ ___ ___ ___ ___ !
    8   6   7   l   3   2   6   5   3   4

One Step Further
How many miles is it from your home to your
school? Ask an adult to help you find out.

Krish

Candy Graph

Directions: Make a **graph** using small colored candies. Put your candies in the correct column on the graphing mat below. Then, color each space on the graph to match the candy that you put on it. Answer the questions at the bottom of the page.

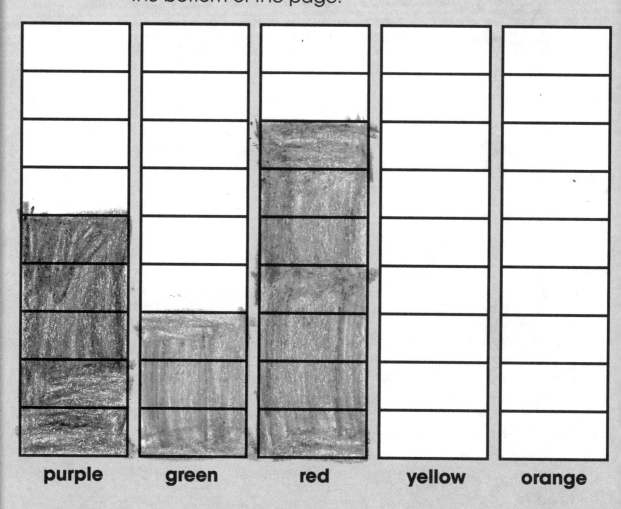

| **purple** | **green** | **red** | **yellow** | **orange** |

Which color do you have the most of? _____

Which color do you have the fewest of? _____

How many candies do you have altogether? _____

One Step Further

Ask a friend to make the same graph.
Is your friend's graph the same as yours?

Turtle Spots

Directions: Count the spots on the turtles. Color the boxes to show how many spots each turtle has.

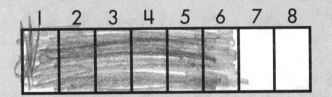

| 1 | 2 | 3 | 4 | 5 | 6 | 7 | 8 |

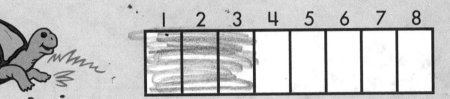

| 1 | 2 | 3 | 4 | 5 | 6 | 7 | 8 |

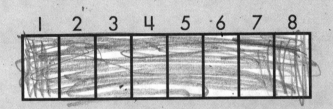

| 1 | 2 | 3 | 4 | 5 | 6 | 7 | 8 |

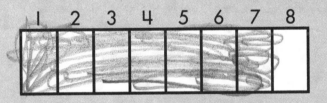

| 1 | 2 | 3 | 4 | 5 | 6 | 7 | 8 |

| 1 | 2 | 3 | 4 | 5 | 6 | 7 | 8 |

One Step Further
Name the turtles on this page.
Which one do you think would win in a race?

Everyday Success First Grade

Take a Bite!

Directions: Count the apples in each row. Color the boxes to show how many apples have bites taken out of them.

Example:

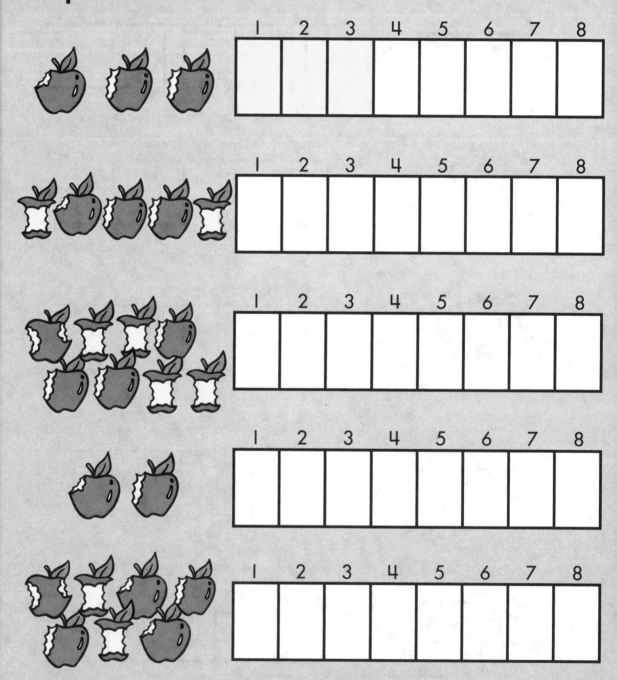

One Step Further

Eat an apple. How many bites does it take you to eat the whole apple?

Wormy Apples

Directions: Color the boxes to show how many worms are in each apple. Answer the questions at the bottom of the page.

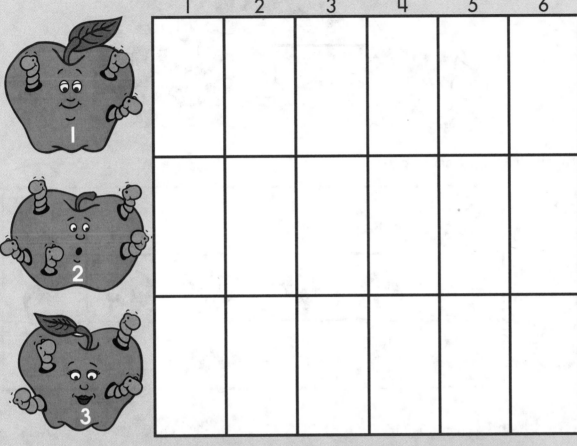

| | 1 | 2 | 3 | 4 | 5 | 6 |

How many worms are in apple 1? _____

How many worms are in apple 2? _____

How many worms are in apple 3? _____

How many more worms are in apple 2 than apple 3? _____

How many fewer worms are in apple 1 than apple 2? _____

One Step Further
Give an apple to your favorite teacher.
Tell him or her what you like about school.

Catfishing

Graphing

I go fishing every Saturday!

This picture graph shows how many fish Cat caught.

First Saturday	fish	fish	fish			
Second Saturday	fish	fish	fish	fish	fish	fish
Third Saturday	fish	fish	fish	fish		

Directions: Look at the graph and answer the questions below.

1. How many fish did Cat catch on the first Saturday? _____

2. How many more fish did he catch the next Saturday? _____

3. On which Saturday did Cat catch the most fish? _____

4. On which Saturday did Cat catch the fewest fish? _____

5. How many fish did Cat catch altogether? _____

One Step Further
What do you do every Saturday?
What do you do every Monday?

Honey Bear's Bakery

Directions: Color a space in the graph to show how many of each treat are in the bakery.

Number of Bakery Treats

12						
11						
10						
9						
8						
7						
6						
5						
4						
3						
2						
1						

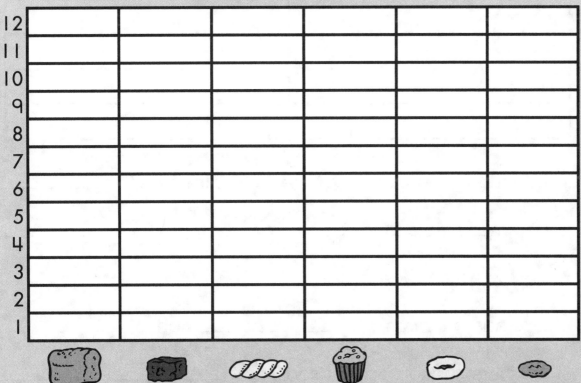

One Step Further

Name your favorite bakery treat. Which of these treats would you like to buy?

Everyday Success First Grade

Amy's Things

Directions: Count the toys on Amy's shelf. Complete the table. Then, answer the questions.

Toy	How Many?

1. How many books and pigs are there altogether? _____

2. How many more teddy bears are there than cars? _____

3. Are there more dolls or animals? _____

4. Amy has four more _____ than _____.

5. Are there enough cars for each doll? _____

One Step Further
How many kinds of toys are on your toy shelf?
What toy do you have the most of?

Fantastic First Graders

Directions: Complete the table using the information shown. Then, answer the questions.

Class	Boys	Girls	Total
A		17	28
B	12	15	
C	9		23
Total			

Great Job!

1. Which class has the most students? _____

2. Which class has the fewest students? _____

3. How many more girls than boys are in the first grade? _____

4. Which class has the most boys? _____

5. Which class has the fewest girls? _____

6. How many students are in first grade? _____

7. How many more students are in class A than class C? _____

One Step Further
Make a graph of the boys and girls in your class at school.

Everyday Success First Grade

Food Fun

Directions: The table below tells what each animal brought to the picnic. Write the missing numbers.

Animal	Vegetables	Fruits	Total
Skunk	8	6	14
Raccoon	9		17
Squirrel		8	15
Rabbit	6		13
Owl	7		16
Deer		9	18

Directions: Write the name of the animal that answers each question.

1. Who brought the same number of vegetables as fruits? _____

2. Who brought two more fruits than vegetables? _____

3. Who brought two more vegetables than fruits? _____

4. Which two animals brought one more fruit than vegetable?

   _____ and _____

5. Which two animals brought the most vegetables?

   _____ and _____

6. Which two animals brought the most fruits?

   _____ and _____

One Step Further
What fruits and vegetables would you bring to a picnic?

Graphing

Make your own graph.

Here is a happy face:

Here is a sad face:

Directions: Count up the happy and sad faces you see below. Then, answer the questions.

How many happy faces did you count? _____

How many sad faces did you count? _____

How many faces are there in all? _____

One Step Further
Take a picture of yourself making a happy face.

Graphing

Directions: Now, make a graph of the happy and sad faces you counted on page 161. The first row has been done for you. A happy face and a sad face have been drawn in. Fill in the other rows to complete the graph.

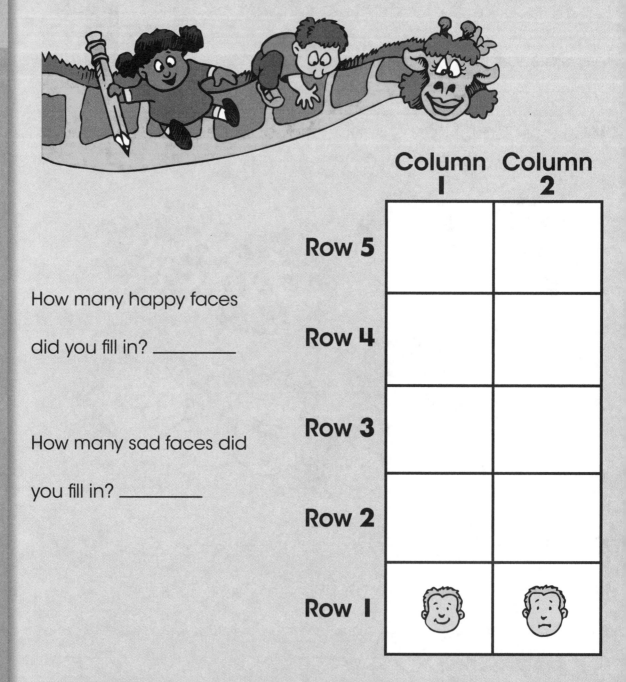

How many happy faces

did you fill in? _____

How many sad faces did

you fill in? _____

One Step Further
Go to a store and watch as people walk by.
Make a graph of faces you see.

Graphing

It's a birthday party! There are lots of good foods to eat.

Directions: Count up all the foods you see.

How many different kinds of food are there? _____

How many egg rolls are there above? _____

How many pizzas did you count? _____

How many cakes did you see? _____

How many tacos are there in all? _____

One Step Further
What foods do you like to eat on your birthday?

MATH

Everyday Success First Grade

Graphing

Directions: Complete the graph below. Use the number of each animal you counted to fill in the rows with the missing pictures of turtles and dogs. The giraffes and sheep have been filled in for you.

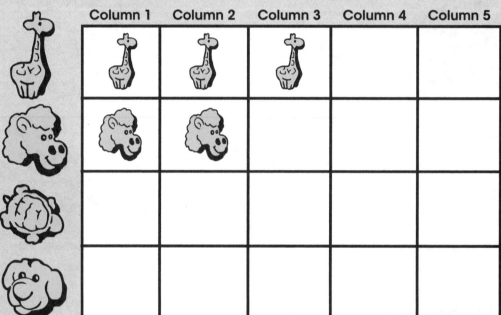

Which animal cracker is there the most of? _____

Which animal cracker is there the fewest of? _____

Three kinds of crackers have the same number.

How many are there? _____

One Step Further
Open a box of animal crackers.
Make a graph of the animals in the box.

Reading

Beginning Consonants: Bb, Cc, Dd, Ff

Beginning consonants are the sounds that come at the beginning of words. Consonants are the letters **b, c, d, f, g, h, j, k, l, m, n, p, q, r, s, t, v, w, x, y,** and **z.**

Consonant Sounds

Directions: Say the name of each letter. Say the sound each letter makes. Circle the letters that make the beginning sound for each picture.

Bb   Cc   Dd   Ff

Bb Dd   Ff Cc   Cc Dd   Ff Bb

Bb Dd   Ff Cc   Cc Dd   Ff Bb

One Step Further
Name a friend or family member whose name starts with the **Bb** sound.

READING

Beginning Consonants: Bb, Cc, Dd, Ff

Directions: Say the name of each letter. Say the sound each letter makes. Draw a line from each letter to the picture that begins with that sound.

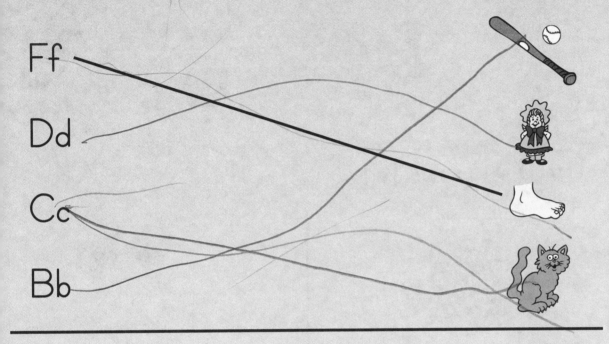

Ff

Dd

Cc

Bb

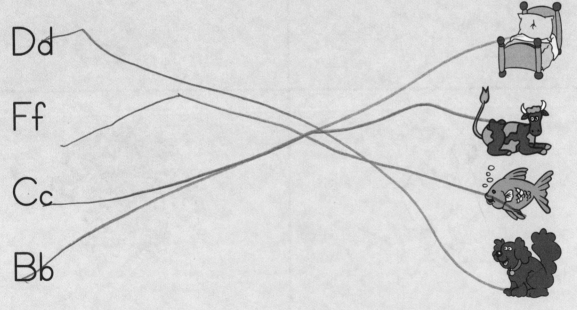

Dd

Ff

Cc

Bb

READING

One Step Further
Find an object in your home that starts with one of the sounds on this page.

Beginning Consonants: Gg, Hh, Jj, Kk

Directions: Say the name of each letter. Say the sound each letter makes. Trace the letter pair that makes the beginning sound in each picture.

Gg   Hh   Jj   Kk

Kk   Hh

Gg   Kk

Gg   Hh

Jj   Gg

One Step Further

Name an animal that starts with the sound of **Gg, Hh, Jj,** or **Kk**.

Beginning Consonants: Gg, Hh, Jj, Kk

Directions: Say the name of each letter. Say the sound each letter makes. Draw a line from each letter pair to the picture that begins with that sound.

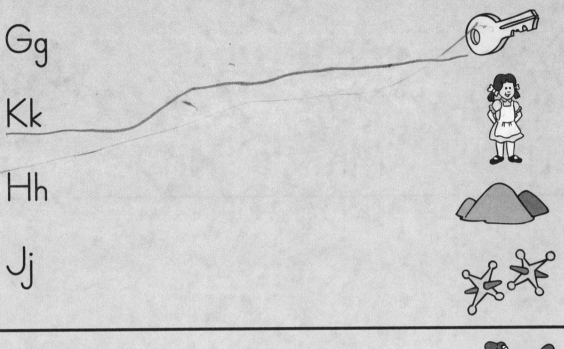

Gg

Kk

Hh

Jj

Kk

Hh

Jj

Gg

One Step Further
Look at a globe. Find a country that starts with one of the sounds on this page.

Everyday Success First Grade

READING

Beginning Consonants: Ll, Mm, Nn, Pp

Directions: Say the name of each letter. Say the sound each letter makes. Trace the letters. Then, draw a line from each letter pair to the picture that begins with that sound.

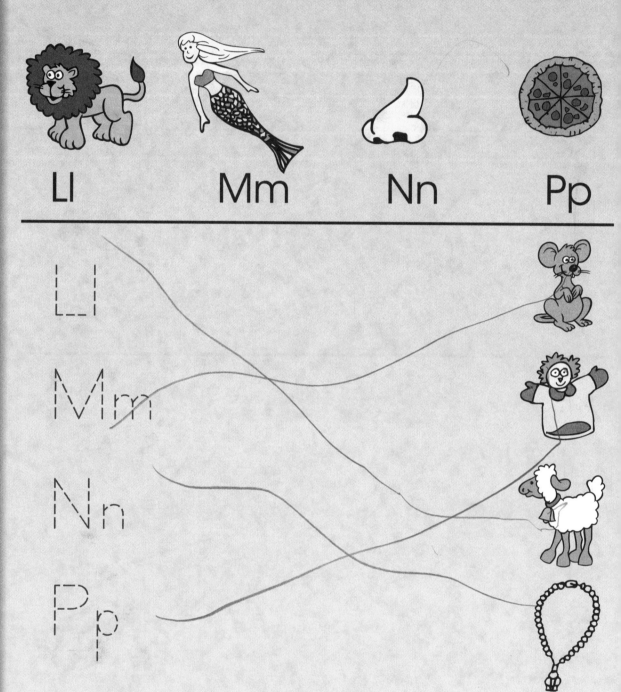

Ll   Mm   Nn   Pp

One Step Further
Name a state or country that starts with the sound of **Ll**, **Mm**, **Nn**, or **Pp**.

Beginning Consonants: Ll, Mm, Nn, Pp

Directions: Say the name of each letter. Say the sound each letter makes. Trace the letter pair that makes the beginning sound in each picture.

Ll   Mm   Nn   Pp

Mm   Ll

Mm   Pp

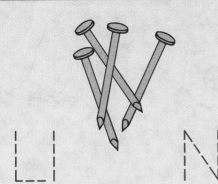

Ll   Nn

Pp   Mm

One Step Further
Draw a map of your state. Mark the city where you live in the right spot on the map.

Everyday Success First Grade

Beginning Consonants: Qq, Rr, Ss, Tt

Directions: Say the name of each letter. Say the sound each letter makes. Trace the letter pair in the boxes. Then, color the picture that begins with that sound.

Qq   Rr   Ss   Tt

Tt

Qq

Rr   Ss

One Step Further

Name another animal that starts with the
Tt sound.

Beginning Consonants: Qq, Rr, Ss, Tt

Directions: Say the name of each letter. Say the sound each letter makes. Draw a line from each letter pair to the picture that begins with that sound.

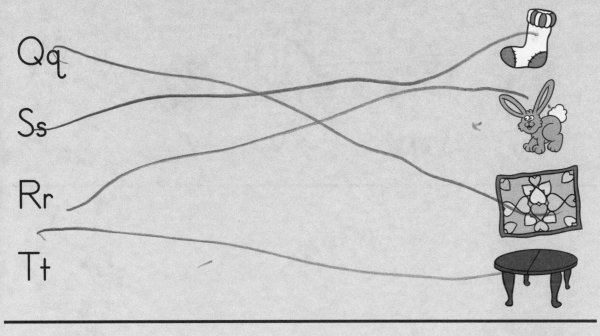

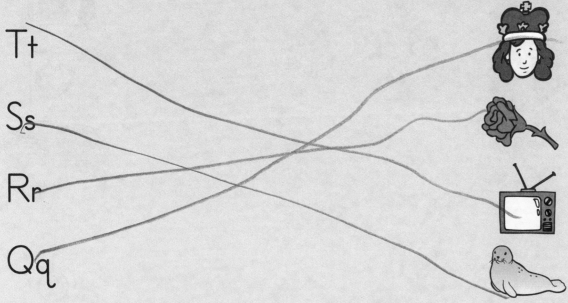

One Step Further
Find an object in your school that starts with one of the sounds on this page.

Beginning Consonants: Vv, Ww, Xx, Yy, Zz

Directions: Say the name of each letter. Say the sound each letter makes. Trace the letters. Then, draw a line from each letter pair to the picture that begins with that sound.

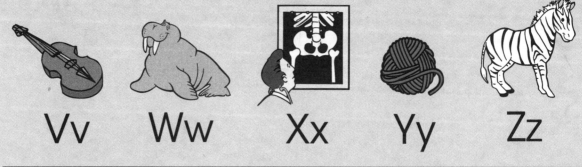

Vv   Ww   Xx   Yy   Zz

Vv

Ww

Xx

Yy

Zz

One Step Further
Make a valentine and give it to a friend.
Include words that start with the **Vv** sound.

Beginning Consonants: Vv, Ww, Xx, Yy, Zz

Directions: Say the name of each letter. Say the sound each letter makes. Then, draw a line from each letter pair to the picture that begins with that sound.

Vv

Zz

Xx

Yy

Ww

Vv

Zz

Yy

Ww

Xx

READING

One Step Further
Do you know how to play a musical instrument? What would you like to play?

Everyday Success First Grade

Ending Consonants: b, d, f

Directions: Say the name of each picture. Then, write the letter that makes the ending sound for each picture.

b   f   d

b   d   f

f   d   f

b   d   b

One Step Further

What sound does your first name end with?
What sound does your last name end with?

A

Ending Consonants: g, m, n

Directions: Say the name of each picture. Draw a line from each letter to the pictures that end with that sound.

g

m

n

g

m

n

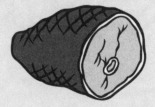

One Step Further

Choose an object outside. Say its name. What sound does the word end with?

Everyday Success First Grade

Ending Consonants: k, l, p

Directions: Trace the letters in each row. Say the name of each picture. Then, color the pictures in each row that end with that sound.

READING

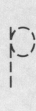    

One Step Further

How many of the objects on this page can
you find in your home?

Ending Consonants: r, s, t, x

Directions: Say the name of each picture. Then, circle the ending sound for each picture.

   r s t x

   r s t x

   r s t x

   r s t x

   r s t x

   r s t x

   r s t x

   r s t x

READING

One Step Further
Ask a friend to name several objects.
What is the ending sound for each word?

Everyday Success First Grade

Consonant Review

Consonant Sounds

Directions: One letter is missing in each word. Write the missing letter on the line.

og   bo   un

he   tu ip   op

lo   lea   wa on

One Step Further
Draw a picture of something in your home.
Write the name of the object you drew.

Consonant Review

Directions: Write all the missing consonants.

a

o

i

e

a

a e

oa

a

a

READING

One Step Further
What state do you live in? Which consonants are in the name of your state?

Meet Short a

Vowel
Sounds

Listen for the sound of short **a** in **van**.

 van

Directions: Trace the letter. Write it on the line.

Directions: Color the pictures whose names have the short **a** sound.

**Vowel
Sounds**

READING

One Step Further
How many words can you name that rhyme
with **cat**? Do they have the short **a** sound?

Short a Maze

Directions: Help the cat get to the bag. Connect all the pictures whose names have the short **a** sound from the cat to the bag.

One Step Further
Draw more objects that have the short **a** sound.

Meet Short e

Listen for the sound of short **e** in **hen**.

hen

Directions: Trace the letter. Write it on the line.

Directions: Color the pictures whose names have the short **e** sound.

One Step Further
Tell a story about a hen. What words in your story have the short **e** sound?

A Matching Game

Directions: Draw a line to connect each picture with its matching short **e** word.

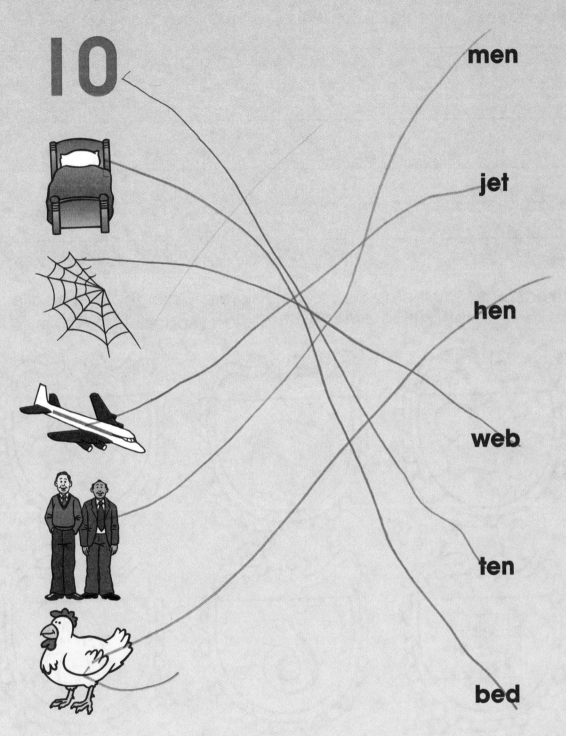

men

jet

hen

web

ten

bed

One Step Further
What words rhyme with the short **e** words on this page?

Meet Short i

Listen for the sound of short **i** in **pig**.

Directions: Trace the letter. Write it on the line.

 pig

I

i

Directions: Say the name of each picture. Color the trim on the bib if the name has the short **i** sound.

One Step Further

Name six words that have the short **i** sound.
Think of rhyming words if you have to.

READING

Read and Color Short i

Directions: Say the name of each picture. Color the pictures whose names have the short **i** sound. The words in the box will give you hints.

milk	crib	bib
pig	kitten	fish

One Step Further
Tell a story about what is happening in the picture.

Meet Short o

Listen for the sound of short **o** in **fox**.

Directions: Trace the letter. Write it on the line.

fox

Directions: Say the name of each picture. Write **o** under the picture if the name has the short **o** sound.

One Step Further
Look around your home for objects with the short **o** sound and put them in a box.

Find Short o Words

Directions: Draw a line under each picture whose name has the short **o** sound.

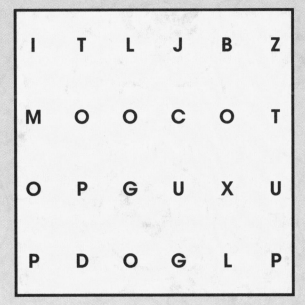

Directions: The words that match the underlined pictures above are hidden in this puzzle. Circle the words. They may go **across** or **down**.

```
I   T   L   J   B   Z

M   O   O   C   O   T

O   P   G   U   X   U

P   D   O   G   L   P
```

READING

One Step Further
Create your own word search puzzle using words you've learned in this book.

Meet Short u

Listen for the sound of short **u** in **bug**.

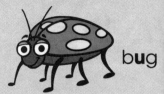
bug

Directions: Trace the letter. Write it on the line.

U

U

Directions: Say the name of each picture. Color the sun yellow if you hear the short **u** sound in the name.

One Step Further
Snug as a bug in a rug! Snuggle under a blanket and read a book.

Short u Tic-Tac-Toe

Directions: Color the pictures whose names have the short **u** sound. Then, play tic-tac-toe. Draw a line through three colored pictures in a row.

One Step Further
Play a game of tic-tac-toe with a friend.
The winner should name a short **u** word.

Meet Long a

Listen for the sound of long **a** in **cake**.

Directions: Color the pictures whose names have the long **a** sound.

cake

One Step Further
What vowels does your name contain?
Are they long or short vowels?

Meet Long e

Listen for the sound of long **e** in **bee**. The letters **ee** and **ea** usually stand for the long **e** sound.

b**ee**

Directions: Write the name of the picture on the correct line.

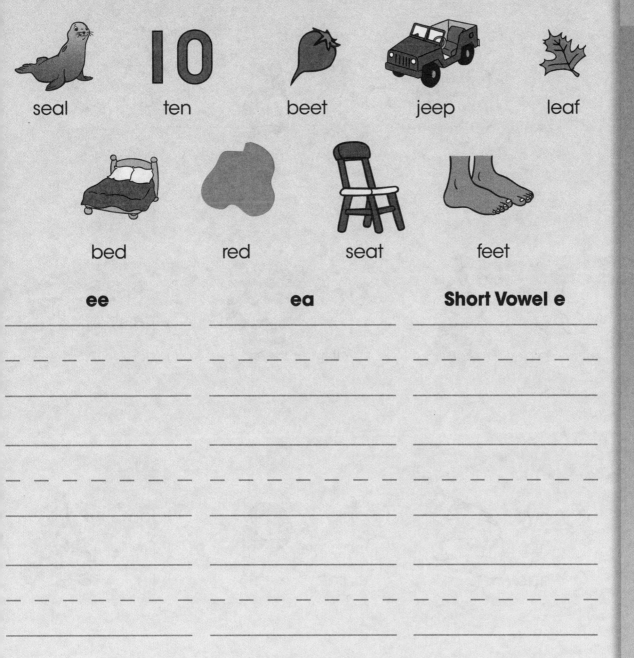

seal   ten   beet   jeep   leaf

bed   red   seat   feet

ee	ea	Short Vowel e

READING

One Step Further
Can you think of other words that contain the long **e** sound?

Everyday Success First Grade

Meet Long i

Listen for the sound of long **i** in **bike**. Look for **i__e**.

Directions: Fill in the circle beside the name of the picture.

bi**k**e

- ○ dim
- ○ date
- ○ dime

- ○ five
- ○ fix
- ○ fame

- ○ kite
- ○ cat
- ○ kit

- ○ pane
- ○ pin
- ○ pine

- ○ tin
- ○ tire
- ○ tale

- ○ red
- ○ ride
- ○ rid

- ○ hive
- ○ hid
- ○ had

- ○ nip
- ○ name
- ○ nine

- ○ fame
- ○ fire
- ○ fin

One Step Further
What words rhyme with the words you
circled? Do they have the short **i** sound, too?

Meet Long o

Listen for the sound of long **o** in **rose**.

Directions: Say the name of each picture. Decide whether the vowel sound you hear is long **o** or short **o**. Fill in the circle beside long **o** or short **o**.

 rose

○ Long o
○ Short o

○ Long o
○ Short o

○ Long o
○ Short o

○ Long o
○ Short o

○ Long o
○ Short o

○ Long o
○ Short o

○ Long o
○ Short o

○ Long o
○ Short o

○ Long o
○ Short o

○ Long o
○ Short o

○ Long o
○ Short o

○ Long o
○ Short o

One Step Further
Make up a story. Use at least four of the objects you see on this page.

Meet Long u

Listen for the sound of long **u** in **mule**. The letters **u__e** and **ue** usually stand for the long **u** sound.

Directions: Circle the pictures whose names have the long **u** sound.

 mule

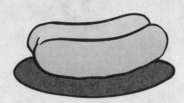

One Step Further
Name your favorite color.
What vowel sound does it contain?

Super Silent e

When you add an **e** to the end of some words, the vowel changes from a short vowel sound to a long vowel sound. The **e** is silent.

Example: rip + **e** = ripe

Directions: Say the word under the first picture in each pair. Then, add an **e** to the word under the next picture. Say the new word.

can _____

tub _____

man _____

kit _____

pin _____

cap _____

One Step Further
Name a three-letter word. Does adding a silent **e** to the end create a brand new word?

Everyday Success First Grade

Words With Silent e

When a silent **e** appears at the end of a word, you can't hear it, but it makes the other vowel have a **long** sound. For example, **tub** has a **short** vowel sound, and **tube** has a **long** vowel sound.

Directions: Look at the pictures below. Decide if the word has a short or long vowel sound. Circle the correct word. Watch for the silent **e**!

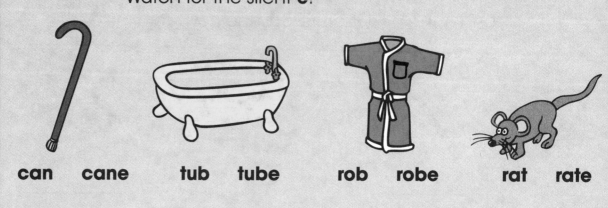

can   cane   tub   tube   rob   robe   rat   rate

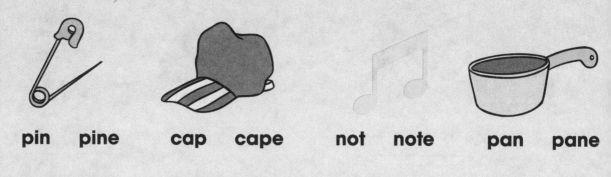

pin   pine   cap   cape   not   note   pan   pane

slid   slide   dim   dime   tap   tape   cub   cube

One Step Further
Look through a book or magazine for more words with silent **e**.

READING

Final y as a Vowel

Our pupp**y** stays dr**y** in the yard.

You know that **y** is a consonant. When **y** is at the beginning of a word, it makes the sound at the beginning of **yard**.

Y can also be a vowel.

Sometimes **y** can have the long **e** sound you hear at the end of **puppy**. **Y** has this sound when it is at the end of a word with more than one syllable or part.

Sometimes **y** can have the long **i** sound you hear at the end of **dry**. **Y** has this sound when it is at the end of a one-syllable word.

Directions: Say each picture name. Circle the word that names the picture. If **y** makes the long **e** sound, color the picture **brown**. If **y** makes the long **i** sound, color the picture **orange**.

bail
bay
baby

crazy
cry
crate

bunt
bunny
buy

fry
frosty
frog

pay
pry
pony

fly
feed
fussy

One Step Further
City ends with a long **e** sound.
What city do you live in?

Which Sound of y?

Directions: Say the name of each picture. If the final **y** stands for the long **e** sound, color the picture **green**. If the **y** stands for the long **i** sound, color the picture yellow.

pony

fly

fifty

candy

dry

penny

cherry

sky

bunny

One Step Further

Name a friend or family member whose name ends in a **y** sound.

Consonant Blends With r

Sometimes two consonants at the beginning of a word blend together. Listen for the **dr** blend in dragon. **Gr, fr, cr, tr, br,** and **pr** are also **r** blends.

dragon

Directions: Draw a line from each consonant blend to the picture whose name begins with the same sound.

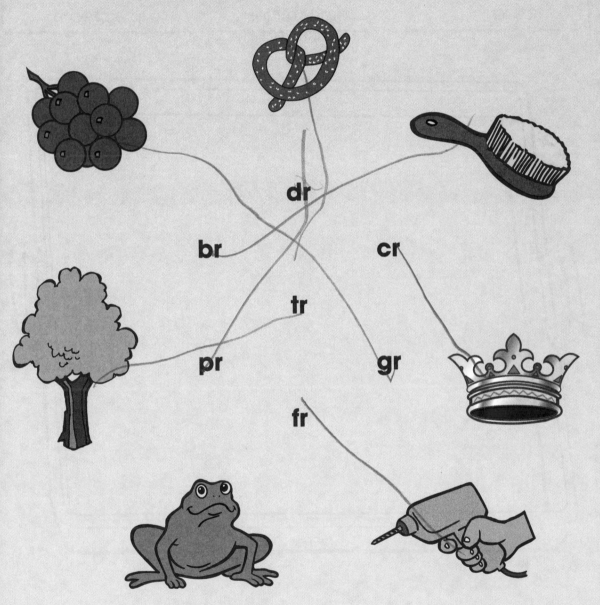

dr

br   cr

tr

pr   gr

fr

READING

One Step Further
Crayon contains a consonant blend with **r**.
Can you name another word?

Fill the Tray

Directions: Read the menu. Circle the words that have **r** blends. On the tray, draw pictures of the foods whose names you circled.

bread	pretzel	meat
butter	milk	grapes
salad	french fries	ice cream

READING

One Step Further

What is your favorite thing to eat for lunch at school?

Consonant Blends With l

Listen for the **cl** blend in clown. **Gl**, **pl**, **fl**, and **bl** are also **l** blends.

Directions: Look at the **l** blend at the beginning of each row. Color the picture whose name begins with that sound.

 **cl**own

bl
  (leaf)

cl
  (crab)

fl

gl

pl
 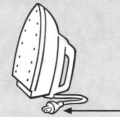 

One Step Further
Clap contains a consonant blend with **l**.
Clap your hands 10 times.

Everyday Success First Grade

Tic-Tac-Toe With l Blends

Directions: Color the pictures whose names begin with **l** blends. Draw a line through three colored pictures in a row to score a tic-tac-toe.

READING

One Step Further

Look at the clock right before you go to sleep. What time does it say?

Consonant Blends With s

Listen for the **sk** blend in **skunk**. **Sm**, **st**, **sp**, **sw**, **sc**, **squ**, **sl**, and **sn** are also **s** blends.

skunk

Directions: Say the name of each picture. Circle the **s** blend you hear at the beginning of the name.

(sn)
sp
st

sw
squ
(sl)

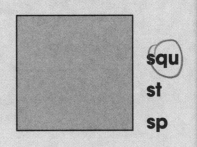
(squ)
st
sp

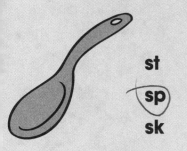
st
(sp)
sk

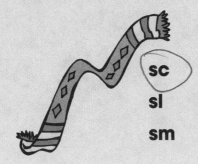
(sc)
sl
sm

squ
sc
(st)

(sw)
st
sm

sm
(sk)
sl

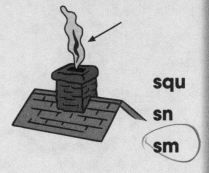
squ
sn
(sm)

One Step Further
Draw a snake. Draw a spoon. What consonant blends do those words contain?

Everyday Success First Grade

Match Pictures and Blends

Directions: Draw a line from each **s** blend to the picture whose name begins with that sound.

squ

sp

sw

sl

sk

sn

st

sm

One Step Further

Lots of words have consonant blends with **s**!
What others can you name?

Blends at the Ends

Some consonant blends come at the ends of words. Listen for the **nd** blend at the end of the word **round**. **Mp**, **ng**, **nt**, **sk**, **nk**, and **st** can also be ending blends.

Directions: Say the name of each picture. Circle the blend you hear at the end of the name.

 rou**nd**

nd
st
(sk)

nt
(nk)
ng

(nt)
st
nd

nd
ng
(mp)

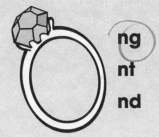
(ng)
nt
nd

nd
(nk)
st

st
(nt)
nd

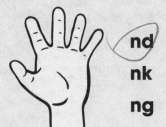
(nd)
nk
ng

(nt)
sk
st

Five

One Step Further
Be very quiet and listen closely. What sounds can you hear around you?

Everyday Success First Grade

Ending Consonant Blends

Directions: Write **lt** or **ft** to complete the words.

be _____

ra _____

sa _____

qui _____

le _____

One Step Further

Does your name contain any consonant blends? Which ones?

Boats

Directions: Read about boats. Then, answer the questions.

See the boats! They float on water. Some boats have sails. The wind moves the sails. It makes the boats go. Many people name their sailboats. They paint the name on the side of the boat.

1. What makes sailboats move? _____

2. Where do sailboats float? _____

3. What would you name a sailboat? _____

READING

One Step Further
Have you ever been on a boat?
Tell a story about riding on a boat.

Tigers

Directions: Read about tigers. Then, answer the questions.

Tigers sleep during the day. They hunt at night. Tigers eat meat. They hunt deer. They like to eat wild pigs. If they cannot find meat on land, tigers will eat fish.

1. When do tigers sleep?   day   night

2. Name two things tigers eat.

_____   _____

- - - - - - - - - - - -   - - - - - - - - - -

_____   _____

3. When do tigers hunt?   day   night

One Step Further
Draw a friend for the tiger.
Name a place you might see a tiger.

READING

Where Flowers Grow

Directions: Read about flowers. Then, answer the questions.

Some flowers grow in pots. Many flowers grow in flower beds. Others grow beside the road. Some flowers begin from seeds. They grow into small buds. Then, they open wide and bloom. Flowers are pretty!

1. Name two places flowers grow.

_____   _____

__ __ __ __ __ __   __ __ __ __ __ __ __ __ __ __ __ __ __

_____   _____

_____

__ __ __ __ __ __ __ __ __ __ __ __ __ __ __

2. Some flowers begin from _____.

_____

__ __ __ __ __ __ __ __ __ __ __ __ __ __ __

3. Then, flowers grow into small _____.

_____

__ __ __ __ __ __ __ __ __ __ __ __ __ __ __

4. Flowers then open wide and _____.

One Step Further
Make a greeting card and include pictures of flowers. Give the card to a friend.

Fish Come in Many Colors

Directions: Read about the color of fish. Then, color the fish.

All fish live in water. Fish that live at the top are **blue**, **green**, or **black**. Fish that live down deep are **silver** or **red**. The colors make it hard to see the fish.

1. Name three colors of fish that live at the top.

2. Name two colors of fish that live down deep.

3. Color the top fish and the bottom fish the correct colors.

One Step Further
Is there a fish tank in your home or school?
What color are the fish that live there?

Zoo Animal Riddles

Directions: Write the name of the animal that answers each riddle.

bear

zebra

lion

camel

elephant

1. I am big and brown. I sleep all winter. What am I? _____

2. I look like a horse with black and white stripes. What am I? _____

3. I have one or two humps on my back. Sometimes people ride on me. What am I? _____

4. I am a very big animal. I have a long nose called a trunk. What am I? _____

5. I have sharp claws and teeth. I am a great big cat. What am I? _____

One Step Further

Which one of these animals would you most like to see? Why?

Important Signs to Know

Directions: Draw a line from the sign to the sentence that tells about it.

1. If you see this sign, watch out for trains.

2. When cars or bikes come to this sign, they must stop.

3. When this sign is on, do not cross the street.

4. This sign tells you to stay out of the yard.

5. If you see this sign, do not eat or drink what is inside!

6. This sign warns you that it is not safe. Stay away!

7. This sign says you are not allowed to come in.

One Step Further
Walk around your neighborhood.
Describe all the signs you see.

Comprehension

Directions: Read the story. Write the words from the story that
complete each sentence.

Jane and Bill like to play in the rain.
They take off their shoes and socks.
They splash in the puddles. It feels
cold! It is fun to splash!

_____

Jane and Bill like to _____.

_____

They take off their _____.

_____

They splash in _____.

Do you like to splash in puddles?   Yes   No

One Step Further
What do you like to do when it rains?
Have you ever played in the rain?

READING

Comprehension

Directions: Read the story. Write the words from the story that complete each sentence.

Ben and Sue have a bug. It is red with black spots. They call it Spot. Spot likes to eat green leaves and grass. The children keep Spot in a box.

READING

_____

_ _

Ben and Sue have a _____

_____

_ _

It is _____ with black spots.

_____

_ _

The bug's name is _____.

_____

_ _

The bug eats _____.

One Step Further

Do you know what kind of bug Spot is? Go outside and try to catch a bug of your own.

What's My Name?

Different words have different jobs. A **naming word** names a person, place, or thing. Naming words are also called **nouns**.

Example: person — nurse
place — store
thing — drum

Directions: In the word box below, circle only the words that name a person, place, or thing. Then, use the nouns you circled to name each picture.

| teacher | up | dog | the | library |
| runs | is | cowboy | cap | zoo |

One Step Further
Name a person, place, and thing in your school.

Everyday Success First Grade

Person, Place, or Thing?

Directions: Write each noun in the correct box below.

girl	school	tree	truck	ball	zoo
artist	park	store	doctor	vase	baby

Person

_____ _____

_____ _____

_____ _____

Place

_____ _____

_____ _____

_____ _____

Thing

_____ _____

_____ _____

_____ _____

One Step Further
What other words could fit into the
Person category?

Finding Nouns

A **noun** names a person, place, or thing.

Directions: Circle two nouns in each sentence below. The first one is done for you.

The (pig) has a curly (tail).

The hen is sitting on her nest.

A horse is in the barn.

The goat has horns.

The cow has a calf.

The farmer is painting the fence.

One Step Further
Ask a friend to write a sentence.
Circle the nouns in that sentence.

Everyday Success First Grade

Nouns at Play

Directions: Complete each sentence with the correct noun from the word box. Write the noun on the line.

ducks	sun	tree
dog	boys	bird

1. A big _____ grows in the park.

2. The _____ is in the sky.

3. A _____ digs a hole.

4. Three _____ swim in the water.

5. A _____ sits on its nest.

6. Two _____ fly a kite.

One Step Further
Read the first sentence of the book nearest you. What are the nouns in that sentence?

Verbs

Directions: Look at the picture and read the words. Write an action word in each sentence below.

1. The two boys like to _____ talk _____ together.

2. The children _____ kick _____ the soccer ball.

3. Some children like to _____ swing _____ on the swing.

4. The girl can _____ hun _____ very fast.

5. The teacher _____ rings _____ the bell.

One Step Further
What other action words do you do on the playground at school?

Ready, Set, Go!

An **action word** tells what a person or thing can do.

Example: Fred **kicks** the ball.

Directions: Read the words below. Circle words that tell what the children are doing.

(jump)
boy

(sleep)
bed

hello
(talk)

(skate)
mittens

(hop)
sidewalk

(sing)
song

(swim)
deep

story
(read)

One Step Further
Name the first thing you do in the morning.
What is the verb?

Action Words

Directions: Underline the action word in each sentence. Then, draw a line to match each sentence with the correct picture. The first one is done for you.

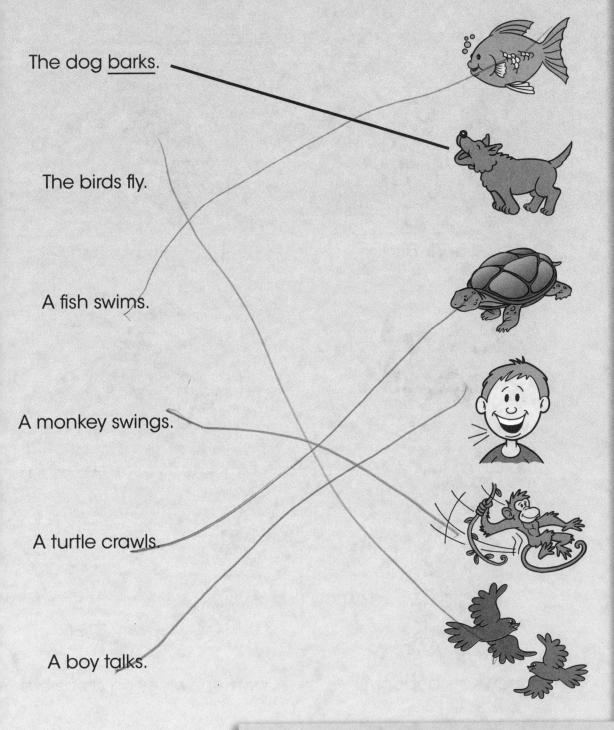

The dog <u>barks</u>.

The birds fly.

A fish swims.

A monkey swings.

A turtle crawls.

A boy talks.

READING

One Step Further
What action words do you do while you are at school?

Verbs

What Is a Verb?

A **verb** is an action word. A verb tells what a person or thing does.

Example: Jane **reads** a book.

Directions: Circle the verb in each sentence below.

Two tiny dogs dance.

The bear climbs a ladder.

The clown falls down.

A tiger jumps through a ring.

A boy eats popcorn.

A woman swings on a trapeze.

One Step Further
Draw a picture of a girl skating in the park.
Go outside and pretend you are skating!

Words That Describe

Directions: Read the words in the box. Choose the word that describes, or tells about, the picture. Write it next to the picture.

wet	round	funny	soft	sad	tall

Soft   tall

funny   Sad

round   wet

One Step Further
Choose an object in your bedroom.
Use three words to describe it.

Everyday Success First Grade

Words That Describe

Directions: Circle the describing word in each sentence. Draw a line from the sentence to the picture.

1. The hungry dog is eating.

2. The tiny bird is flying.

3. Horses have long legs.

4. She is a fast runner.

5. The little boy was lost.

One Step Further
What words could you use to describe yourself?

Adjectives

Describing words are also called **adjectives**.

Directions: Circle the describing words in the sentences.

1. The juicy apple is on the plate.

2. The furry dog is eating a bone.

3. It was a sunny day.

4. The kitten drinks warm milk.

5. The baby has a loud cry.

One Step Further
Describe your favorite subject in school.
What do you like about it?

Everyday Success First Grade

We're the Same!

Words that mean the **same** thing, or close to the same thing, are called **synonyms**.

Directions: Write a word from the word list that has the same meaning as each word below.

bright	hop	dad	fast
pretty	plate	silly	center

 **sunny**

_____

 **beautiful**

_____

 middle

_____

 **dish**

_____

 **quick**

_____

 **jump**

_____

 goofy

_____

 **father**

_____

One Step Further
Begin your day with a healthy breakfast.
What is a synonym for **begin**?

READING

Take My Place

Directions: Choose the word from the word list below that could take the place of the underlined word in each sentence. Write it on the line.

pick	porch	tired	pull	cut	bag

1. I was so <u>sleepy</u>! I couldn't wait to go to bed! _____

2. Please put all your books in this <u>sack</u>. _____

3. Please <u>choose</u> a present you would like to open. _____

4. Are you strong enough to <u>drag</u> this heavy crate? _____

5. "It is important to <u>trim</u> the extra fabric on your art project," said my art teacher. _____

6. We sipped lemonade on the <u>deck</u>. _____

One Step Further
Choose a word from this page.
What word means the opposite of that word?

Antonym Artists!

Antonyms are words that have **opposite** meanings. Abby and Abe are Antonym Artists! They like to draw opposite pictures.

Directions: Help Abe draw the opposite of Abby's pictures.

One Step Further

Draw two more pictures that are antonyms.
What did you draw?

Antonyms are Opposites!

Words with **opposite** meanings are called **antonyms**.

Directions: Circle an antonym for the underlined word in each sentence.

1. The sky was very <u>dark</u>.   purple   old   light

2. Turn <u>left</u> at the light.   right   sideways   yellow

3. The shelf was very <u>high</u>.   pretty   low   loud

4. The turtle walked <u>slowly</u>.   silly   quickly   nicely

5. I <u>whispered</u> at the circus.   laughed   coughed   shouted

6. Bobby is an <u>adult</u>.   child   fan   principal

7. The clown was very <u>strong</u>.   weak   silly   hungry

8. The library is a <u>quiet</u> place.   fun   messy   noisy

READING

One Step Further
Write a sentence. Ask a friend to write a sentence with the opposite meaning.

Batty Bats!

Some words have more than one meaning. The word **bat** has more than one meaning.

Directions: Look at the words and their meanings below. Below each picture, write the number that has the correct meaning.

can: 1. a metal container
2. to know how

_____   _____

band: 1. a group of musicians
2. a strip of material

_____   _____

cap: 1. a soft hat with a visor
2. lid or cover

_____   _____

crow: 1. a large black bird
2. the loud cry of a rooster

_____   _____

One Step Further
Find some cans in your home.
See how high you can stack the cans.

Match That Meaning!

Some words have more than one meaning. Look at the list
of words.

Directions: Match the word's correct meaning to the
pictures below.

cross: 1. to draw a line through
2. angry

fall: 3. the season between summer and winter
4. to trip or stumble

land: 5. to bring to a stop or rest
6. the ground

_____ _____ _____

_____ _____ _____

READING

One Step Further
Can you name another season that has
multiple meanings?

Homonyms

Homonyms are words that sound the same, but are spelled differently and have different meanings. For example, **sun** and **son** are homonyms.

Directions: Look at the word. Circle the picture that goes with the word.

1. sun

2. hi

3. ate

4. four

5. buy

6. hear

One Step Further
What was the last thing you ate?
Name eight of your favorite foods.

Homonyms

Directions: Look at each picture. Circle the homonym that is spelled the correct way.

deer   dear

blue   blew

to   two

hi   high

by   bye

new   knew

red   read

8

ate   eight

One Step Further
What are the last two books you read?
What were the books about?

READING

Everyday Success First Grade

What Will Happen Next?

Directions: Look at the pictures.

Directions: Write what you think will happen next.

_____

_____

One Step Further
Look around your neighborhood. What do you think will happen next?

What's Next?

Directions: Draw a picture of what you think will happen next in the boxes below.

One Step Further
What games do you like to play on the playground?

Critical Thinking

Directions: Use your reading skills to answer each riddle. Unscramble the word to check your answer. Write the correct word on the line.

I am a ruler, but I have two feet, not one.

_____

— — — — — — — —

I am a _____.
(ngik)

I am very bright, but that doesn't make me smart.

_____

— — — — — — — — — —

I am the _____.
(uns)

You can turn me around, but I won't get dizzy.

_____

— — — — — — — —

I am a _____.
(eky)

I can rattle, but I am not a baby's toy.

_____

— — — — — — — —

I am a _____.
(nekas)

I will give you milk, but not in a bottle.

_____

— — — — — — — —

I am a _____.
(ocw)

I smell, but I have no nose.

_____

— — — — — — — —

I am a _____.
(oerflw)

One Step Further
Tell these riddles to a friend.
Did your friend guess the riddles correctly?

Clues About Cats

Directions: Read the clues carefully. Then, number the cats. When you are sure you are correct, color the cats.

1. A **gray** cat sits on the gate.

2. A cat with **orange**-and-**black** spots sits near the tree.

3. A **brown** cat sits near the bush.

4. A **white** cat sits between the **orange**-and-**black** spotted cat and the **gray** cat.

5. A **black** cat sits next to the **brown** cat.

6. An **orange** cat sits between the **gray** cat and the **black** cat.

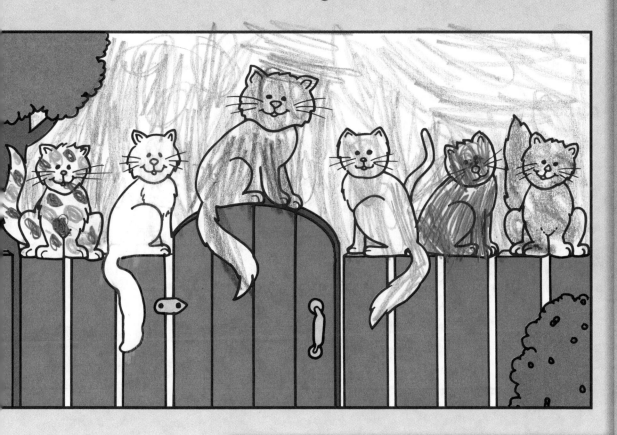

One Step Further
Describe a picture. Ask a friend to draw the picture based on your description.

Everyday Success First Grade

READING

Hey! What's the Big Idea?

Directions: Circle the words that are shown in the picture above.

bowl	spatula	bed	dog	ink
oven	pan	jar	pot	phone
mixer	napkins	scooter	girl	sneakers
mitt	paper	car	socks	cupcake tin
spoon	towels	cat	milk	

Directions: Circle and write the best title for the picture.

Baking With Dad   Chocolate Attack!   Eating Food

_____

Tell why the other two titles are not as good.

_____

_____

One Step Further
Ask an adult to help you bake cupcakes.
Describe the steps you take.

Picture This!

Directions: Look at the picture. Circle and write the best title on the lines below.

B-r-r-r, It's Cold!   Bears and Birds

Asleep for the Winter   Bears Go Shopping

_____

_____

Fishing   Our New Fish

The Pet Store   Fish and Chips

_____

_____

Spring Cleaning   My New Toy

Saturday Fun   New Shoes

_____

_____

One Step Further
Draw a picture about your day at school.
What title do you give the picture?

Everyday Success First Grade

What's the Main Idea?

The **main idea** tells about the **whole picture**.

Directions: Does the sentence tell the main idea of the picture? Circle **yes** or **no**. Then, write the sentence that best states the main idea for each picture.

The cat wants to play.   yes   no

The cat takes a nap.   yes   no

_____

_____

The brothers play together.   yes   no

The brothers are smart.   yes   no

_____

_____

The dog is hungry.   yes   no

The dog is playful.   yes   no

_____

_____

One Step Further
Draw pictures to illustrate all the sentences on this page.

READING

Story Time

The **main idea** tells about the **whole story**.

Read the story below.

"Mom, can we build a fort in the dining room?" John asked.

"Sure, honey," said John's mom. Then, John's mom covered the dining room table with a giant sheet. "Do you want to eat lunch in our fort?" asked John's mom.

"Yes!" said John. Then, John's mom brought two peanut butter sandwiches on paper plates and sat under the table, too!

"Mom, making a fort with you is so much fun!" said John, smiling.

Directions: Does the sentence tell the main idea? Write **yes** or **no**.

1. Then, John's mom covered the dining room table with a giant

   sheet. _____

2. "Do you want to eat lunch in our fort?" asked John's mom.

   _____

3. "Mom, making a fort with you is so much fun!" _____

4. Write a sentence that tells the main idea: _____

   _____

One Step Further
With a friend, build a fort somewhere in your home. What will you do in your fort?

Caitlin Uses Context Clues

When you read, it is important to know about context clues.
Context clues can help you figure out the meaning of a word or a
missing word just by looking at the other words in the sentence.

Example: It was so (hot) outside that I decided I

would go to the (beach) and _____ **swim** _____.
     play   laugh   shovel   swim

"Swim" is the correct answer because of the context
clues "hot" and "beach."

Directions: Read each sentence below. Circle the context clues,
or other words in the sentence that give you hints
about the meaning. Choose the answer that fits in
each blank. Write it on the line.

1. Last night I went to bed very late and now I feel

   _____.
       happy   hungry   tired   yawn

2. When I broke my mom's favorite

   vase she was _____.
       worried   nice   magic   angry

One Step Further
What do you like to do when it's hot outside?
Name your favorite outdoor activity.

Context Clues

Directions: Read each sentence below. Circle the context clues. Choose the answer that fits in each blank. Write it on the line.

1. The cold wind and lack of heat made me wish

   I had an extra _____.
   umbrella   toy   shovel   jacket

2. A whale is a very _____ mammal. Sailors often
   thought whales were actually small islands!
   small   graceful   large   blue

3. Eating fruit is important for _____
   health. Fruit is full of many important vitamins.
   bad   good   okay   cat

4. The bus was very large and had a lot of seats. It could carry

   _____ people.
   few   hungry   many   tired

5. The clown looked very _____
   wearing a tiny pink tutu!
   silly   smart   orange   light

One Step Further
Name everything you do for good health.
Do you eat fruit? Exercise?

Everyday Success First Grade

READING

Carlo's Context Clues

Directions: Read each sentence below. Circle the context clues. Choose a word from the word list to replace each word in **bold**. Write it on the line.

| stop | shined | lively | tease | yummy |

1. This prize-winning chocolate cream pie

   is **delicious**. _____

2. Please do not **taunt** your younger brother. Mean

   words hurt his feelings. _____

3. The police officer told us to **halt** when we came

   to the red traffic light. _____

4. The bouncy, happy puppy was very

   energetic. _____

5. The silver bowl really **gleamed** after you

   polished it. _____

One Step Further
Look at the sentences on this page.
Name an antonym of each word in bold.

Context Clues

Directions: Read each sentence below. Circle the context clues.
Choose a word from the word list to replace each
word in **bold**. Write it on the line.

petted	little	understand	yelled	tell

1. "Don't **reveal** the secret! We want the party to

   be a surprise!" said Mary. _____

2. I can't **grasp** that hard math problem! It is too

   difficult. _____

3. The baby bird was so **tiny** that we could hardly

   see it. _____

4. We **stroked** the soft kitten and heard

   it purr. _____

5. The crowd **hollered** when the player was

   called out. _____

One Step Further
Do something to surprise a friend. Make your
friend a card or give him or her a gift.

Answer Key

Rhyming Words

6 — Rhyming

Rhyming words are words that sound alike at the end of the word. **Cat** and **hat** rhyme.

Directions: Draw a circle around each word pair that rhymes. Draw an **X** on each pair that does **not** rhyme.

Example:

(soap rope)	red dog ✗	(book hook)
cold rock ✗	(cat hat)	yellow black ✗
one two ✗	(rock sock)	(rat flat)
good nice ✗	you to ✗	meet toy ✗
(old sold)	(sale whale)	word letter ✗

One Step Further
Choose two rhyming words from this page. Can you find both objects in your home?

Everyday Success First Grade

Rhyming Words

7 — Rhyming

Rhyming words are words that sound alike at the end of the word.

Directions: Draw a line to match the pictures that rhyme. Write two of your rhyming word pairs below.

Answers may include:

hat   cat
goat   coat

One Step Further
What word rhymes with your name? Make up a word if you have to!

Everyday Success First Grade

ABC Order

8 — ABC Order

Directions: Circle the first letter of each word. Then, put each pair of the words in **ABC** order.

ⓒar   ⓑird   ⓜoon   ⓣwo   ⓝest   ⓕan

bird   moon   fan
car   two   nest

ⓒard   ⓓog   ⓟig   ⓑike   ⓢun   ⓟie

card   bike   pie
dog   pig   sun

One Step Further
Write three words. Ask a friend to put them in ABC order.

Everyday Success First Grade

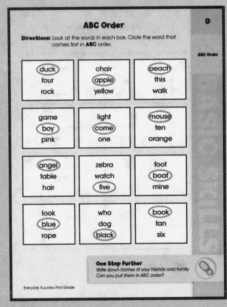

ABC Order

9 — ABC Order

Directions: Look at the words in each box. Circle the word that comes first in **ABC** order.

(duck) four rock	chair (apple) yellow	(peach) this walk
game (boy) pink	light (come) one	(mouse) ten orange
(angel) table hair	zebra watch (five)	foot (boat) mine
look (blue) rope	who dog (black)	(book) tan six

One Step Further
Write down names of your friends and family. Can you put them in ABC order?

Everyday Success First Grade

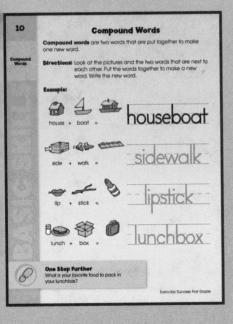

Compound Words

10 — Compound Words

Compound words are two words that are put together to make one new word.

Directions: Look at the pictures and the two words that are next to each other. Put the words together to make a new word. Write the new word.

Example:

house + boat = houseboat

side + walk = sidewalk

lip + stick = lipstick

lunch + box = lunchbox

One Step Further
What is your favorite food to pack in your lunchbox?

Everyday Success First Grade

Compound Words

11 — Compound Words

Directions: Circle the compound word that completes each sentence. Write each word on the lines.

1. The mailman brings us letters.
(mailman) snowman

2. A sunflower grows tall.
sunlight (sunflower)

3. The snow falls outside.
(outside) inside

4. A raindrop fell on my head.
(raindrop) rainbow

5. I put the letter in a mailbox.
(mailbox) shoebox

One Step Further
Write a letter to a friend. Put it in the mailbox or give it to the mailman to send.

Everyday Success First Grade

ANSWER KEY

Names

12

Names

You are a special person. Your name begins with a capital letter. We put a capital letter at the beginning of people's names because they are special.

Directions: Write your name. Did you remember to use a capital letter?

Answers will vary.

Directions: Write each person's name. Use a capital letter at the beginning.

Ted — Ted
Katie — Katie
Mike — Mike
Tim — Tim

One Step Further
Write the names of your family members. How many people are in your family?

Everyday Success First Grade

Days of the Week

13

Names

The days of the week begin with capital letters.

Directions: Write the days of the week in the spaces below. Put them in order. Be sure to start with capital letters.

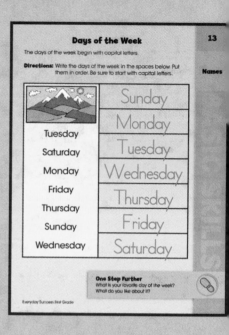

	Sunday
Tuesday	Monday
Saturday	Tuesday
Monday	Wednesday
Friday	Thursday
Thursday	Friday
Sunday	Saturday
Wednesday	

One Step Further
What is your favorite day of the week? What do you like about it?

Everyday Success First Grade

Months of the Year

14

Names

The months of the year begin with capital letters.

Directions: Write the months of the year in order on the calendar below. Be sure to start with capital letters.

January	December	April	May
October	June	September	February
July	March	November	August

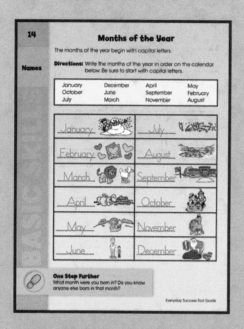

January	July
February	August
March	September
April	October
May	November
June	December

One Step Further
What month were you born in? Do you know anyone else born in that month?

Everyday Success First Grade

More Than One

15

More Than One

Directions: An **s** at the end of a word often means there is more than one. Look at each picture. Circle the correct word. Write the word on the line.

two dog (dogs) — dogs
four flower (flowers) — flowers
one bikes (bike) — bike
three (toys) toy — toys
a (lamb) lambs — lamb
two cat (cats) — cats

One Step Further
Name something you own more than one of. How many do you own of that object?

Everyday Success First Grade

More Than One

16

More Than One

Directions: Read the nouns under the pictures. Then, write each noun under **One** or **More Than One**.

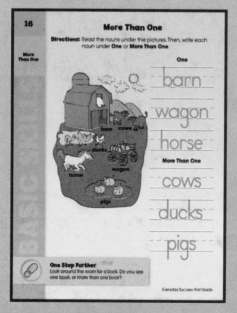

barn, cows, ducks, horse, wagon, pigs

One
barn
wagon
horse

More Than One
cows
ducks
pigs

One Step Further
Look around the room for a book. Do you see one book, or more than one book?

Everyday Success First Grade

More Than One

17

More Than One

Directions: Choose the word that completes each sentence. Write each word on the line.

1. I have a __dog__
   dog / dogs

2. Four __apples__ are on the tree.
   apple / apples

3. I read two __books__ today.
   book / books

4. My __bike__ is blue.
   bike / bikes

5. We saw lots of __monkeys__ at the zoo.
   monkey / monkeys

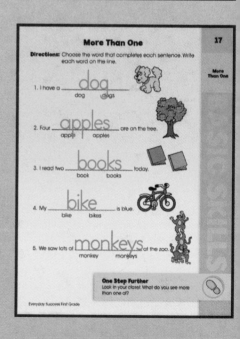

One Step Further
Look in your closet. What do you see more than one of?

Everyday Success First Grade

Everyday Success First Grade

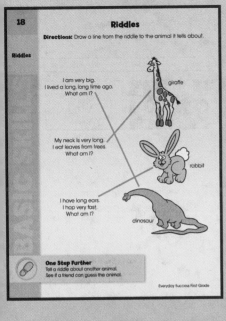

18 Riddles

Directions: Draw a line from the riddle to the animal it tells about.

I am very big. I lived a long, long time ago. What am I?

My neck is very long. I eat leaves from trees. What am I?

I have long ears. I hop very fast. What am I?

giraffe

rabbit

dinosaur

One Step Further
Tell a riddle about another animal. See if a friend can guess the animal.

Everyday Success First Grade

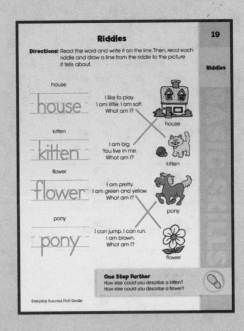

Riddles 19

Directions: Read the word and write it on the line. Then, read each riddle and draw a line from the riddle to the picture it tells about.

house — house
kitten — kitten
flower — flower
pony — pony

I like to play. I am little. I am soft. What am I? (house)
I am big. You live in me. What am I? (kitten)
I am pretty. I am green and yellow. What am I? (pony)
I can jump. I can run. I am brown. What am I? (flower)

One Step Further
How else could you describe a kitten? How else could you describe a flower?

Everyday Success First Grade

20 Riddles

Directions: Write a word from the box to answer each riddle.

sundae   book   chair   sun

There are many words in me. I am fun to read. What am I? **book**

I am soft and yellow. You can sit on me. What am I? **chair**

I am in the sky in the day. I am hot. I am yellow. What am I? **sun**

I am cold. I am sweet. You like to eat me. What am I? **sundae**

One Step Further
Choose an object at school. Describe the object and ask a friend to guess.

Everyday Success First Grade

These Keep Me Warm 21

Directions: Color the things that keep you warm.

socks, apple, lunch box, earmuffs, cookie, coat, umbrella, hat, gloves, book

One Step Further
What do you do when you are cold? What clothes do you wear during the winter?

Everyday Success First Grade

22 Things to Drink

Directions: Circle the pictures of things you can drink. Write the names of those things in the blanks.

milk, ice, soup and crackers
juice, soda, ice-cream bar

milk   soda   juice

One Step Further
Name something else you can drink. What is your favorite thing to drink?

Everyday Success First Grade

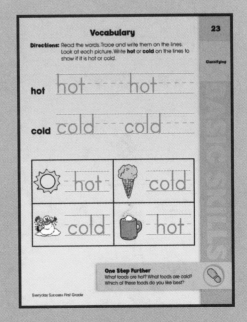

Vocabulary 23

Directions: Read the words. Trace and write them on the lines. Look at each picture. Write **hot** or **cold** on the lines to show if it is hot or cold.

hot — hot — hot
cold — cold — cold

sun: hot
ice cream: cold
snowman: cold
mug: hot

One Step Further
What foods are hot? What foods are cold? Which of these foods do you like best?

Everyday Success First Grade

Everyday Success First Grade

ANSWER KEY

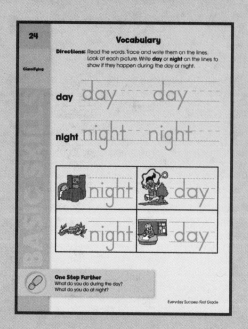

24 — Vocabulary

Directions: Read the words. Trace and write them on the lines. Look at each picture. Write **day** or **night** on the lines to show if they happen during the day or night.

Classifying

day — day   day

night — night   night

night	day
night	day

One Step Further
What do you do during the day?
What do you do at night?

Everyday Success First Grade

25 — Night and Day

Directions: Write the words from the box under the pictures they describe.

Classifying

stars sun moon rays dark light night day

stars	sun
moon	rays
dark	light
night	day

One Step Further
How do you know when it's nighttime?
Describe how you can tell.

Everyday Success First Grade

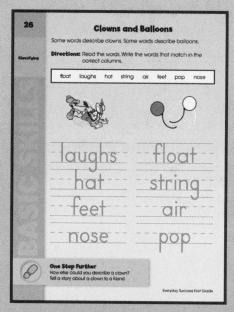

26 — Clowns and Balloons

Some words describe clowns. Some words describe balloons.

Directions: Read the words. Write the words that match in the correct columns.

Classifying

float laughs hat string air feet pop nose

laughs	float
hat	string
feet	air
nose	pop

One Step Further
How else could you describe a clown?
Tell a story about a clown to a friend.

Everyday Success First Grade

27 — Similarities

Directions: Circle the picture in each row that is most like the first picture. What is similar about the two objects?

Classifying

Example:

potato   rose   tomato   tree

shirt   mittens   boots   (jacket)

tiger   giraffe   (lion)   zebra

One Step Further
Find two objects in your room that go together. Describe their similarities.

Everyday Success First Grade

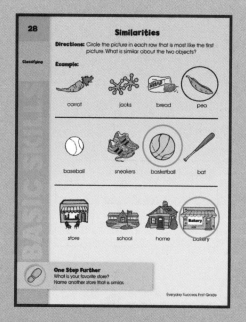

28 — Similarities

Directions: Circle the picture in each row that is most like the first picture. What is similar about the two objects?

Classifying

Example:

carrot   jacks   bread   pea

baseball   sneakers   (basketball)   bat

store   school   home   (bakery)

One Step Further
What is your favorite store?
Name another store that is similar.

Everyday Success First Grade

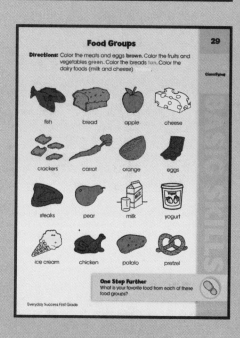

29 — Food Groups

Directions: Color the meats and eggs brown. Color the fruits and vegetables green. Color the breads tan. Color the dairy foods (milk and cheese).

Classifying

fish   bread   apple   cheese

crackers   carrot   orange   eggs

steaks   pear   milk   yogurt

ice cream   chicken   potato   pretzel

One Step Further
What is your favorite food from each of these food groups?

Everyday Success First Grade

30 — Things That Belong Together

Classifying

Directions: Circle the pictures in each row that belong together.

Row 1: cookies, cake, beans, ice cream
Row 2: kite, dice, checkers, chess

Directions: Write the names of the things that do **not** belong. Why do these pictures not belong?

Row 1: beans
Row 2: kite

One Step Further
Name a game you can play on a rainy day. Draw it here.

Everyday Success First Grade

31 — What Does Not Belong?

Classifying

Directions: Draw an **X** on the picture that does **not** belong in each group.

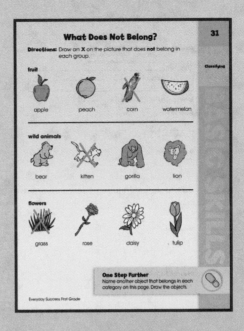

fruit: apple, peach, corn, watermelon
wild animals: bear, kitten, gorilla, lion
flowers: grass, rose, daisy, tulip

One Step Further
Name another object that belongs in each category on this page. Draw the objects.

Everyday Success First Grade

32 — What Does Not Belong?

Classifying

Directions: Draw an **X** on the word in each row that does **not** belong.

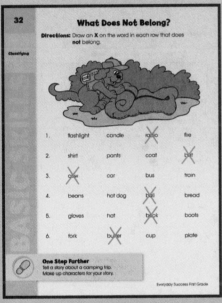

1. flashlight, candle, radio, fire
2. shirt, pants, coat, hat
3. claw, car, bus, train
4. beans, hot dog, ball, bread
5. gloves, hat, book, boots
6. fork, butter, cup, plate

One Step Further
Tell a story about a camping trip. Make up characters for your story.

Everyday Success First Grade

33 — Things That Belong Together

Classifying

Directions: Circle the pictures in each row that belong together.

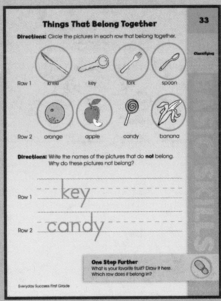

Row 1: knife, key, fork, spoon
Row 2: orange, apple, candy, banana

Directions: Write the names of the pictures that do **not** belong. Why do these pictures not belong?

Row 1: key
Row 2: candy

One Step Further
What is your favorite fruit? Draw it here. Which row does it belong in?

Everyday Success First Grade

34 — Why They Are Different

Classifying

Directions: Look at your answers on page 33. Write why each object does not belong.

Row 1: Cannot eat with a key.
Row 2: Candy is not a fruit.

Directions: For each object, draw a group of pictures that belong with it.

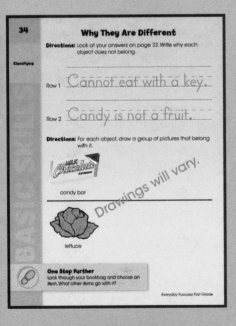

candy bar

lettuce

Drawings will vary.

One Step Further
Look through your bookbag and choose an item. What other items go with it?

Everyday Success First Grade

35 — What Does Not Belong?

Classifying

Directions: Circle the two things that do not belong in the picture. Write why they do not belong.

1. Flowers do not grow in snow.
2. Palm trees do not grow in snow.

One Step Further
Describe what is happening in the picture. What winter activities do you enjoy?

Everyday Success First Grade

Everyday Success First Grade

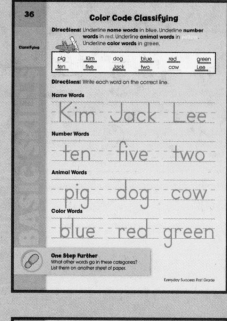

36 Color Code Classifying

Classifying

Directions: Underline **name words** in blue. Underline **number words** in red. Underline **animal words** in yellow. Underline **color words** in green.

pig	Kim	dog	blue	red	green
ten	five	Jack	two	cow	Lee

Directions: Write each word on the correct line.

Name Words
Kim Jack Lee

Number Words
ten five two

Animal Words
pig dog cow

Color Words
blue red green

One Step Further
What other words go in these categories?
List them on another sheet of paper.

Everyday Success First Grade

Menu Mix-Up 37

Classifying

Directions: Circle names of **drinks** in red. Circle names of **vegetables** in green. Circle names of **desserts** in pink.

Directions: Write each food word on the correct line.

Drinks	Vegetables	Desserts
water	corn	cookie
juice	peas	pie
milk	carrot	cake

One Step Further
Pretend you own a restaurant.
What would be on your menu?

Everyday Success First Grade

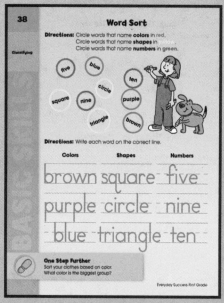

38 Word Sort

Classifying

Directions: Circle words that name **colors** in red. Circle words that name **shapes** in blue. Circle words that name **numbers** in green.

Directions: Write each word on the correct line.

Colors	Shapes	Numbers
brown	square	five
purple	circle	nine
blue	triangle	ten

One Step Further
Sort your clothes based on color.
What color is the biggest group?

Everyday Success First Grade

Where Does It Belong? 39

Classifying

Directions: Read the words.
Draw a **circle** around the **sky words**.
Draw a **line** under the **land words**.
Draw a **box** around the **sea words**.

city	rabbit	planet
cloud	forest	whale
shark	moon	shell

Directions: Write each word on the correct line.

Sky Words
cloud moon planet

Land Words
city rabbit forest

Sea Words
shark whale shell

One Step Further
Walk around your neighborhood.
What other land words could you add?

Everyday Success First Grade

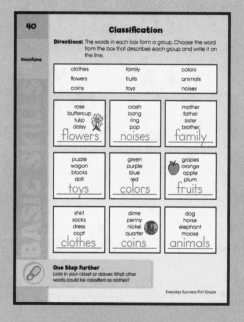

40 Classification

Classifying

Directions: The words in each box form a group. Choose the word from the box that describes each group and write it on the line.

clothes	family	colors
flowers	fruits	animals
coins	toys	noises

rose buttercup tulip daisy	crash bang ring pop	mother father sister brother
flowers	**noises**	**family**

puzzle wagon blocks doll	green purple blue red	grapes orange apple plum
toys	**colors**	**fruits**

shirt socks dress coat	dime penny nickel quarter	dog horse elephant moose
clothes	**coins**	**animals**

One Step Further
Look in your closet or drawer. What other words could be classified as clothes?

Everyday Success First Grade

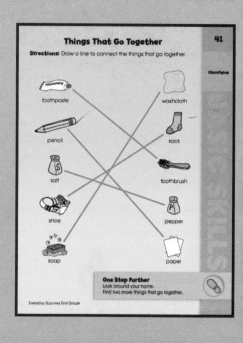

Things That Go Together 41

Classifying

Directions: Draw a line to connect the things that go together.

toothpaste — washcloth
pencil — sock
salt — toothbrush
shoe — pepper
soap — paper

One Step Further
Look around your home.
Find two more things that go together.

Everyday Success First Grade

Everyday Success First Grade

42 — Things That Go Together

Directions: Draw a line to connect the things that go together.

Classifying

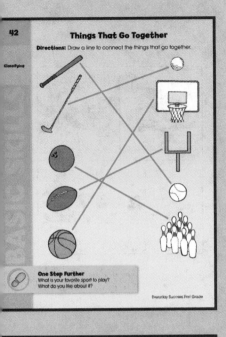

One Step Further
What is your favorite sport to play?
What do you like about it?

Everyday Success First Grade

43 — Raking Leaves

Directions: Write a number in each box to show the order of the story.

Sequencing

One Step Further
Go outside and find 10 leaves.
What color are the leaves?

Everyday Success First Grade

44 — Make a Snowman!

Directions: Write the number of the sentence that goes with each picture in the box.

Sequencing

1. Roll a large snowball for the snowman's bottom.
2. Make another snowball and put it on top of the first.
3. Put the last snowball on top.
4. Dress the snowman.

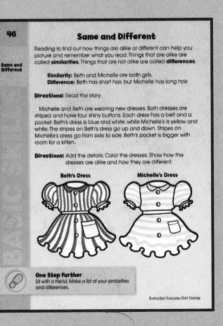

One Step Further
Tell a story about building a snowman.
Have you ever built a snowman?

Everyday Success First Grade

45 — How Flowers Grow

Directions: Read the story. Then, write the steps to grow a flower.

Sequencing

First, find a sunny spot. Then, plant the seed. Water it. The flower will start to grow. Pull the weeds around it. Remember to keep giving the flower water. Enjoy your flower.

1. Find a sunny spot.
2. Plant the seed.
3. Water it.
4. Pull the weeds.
5. Enjoy your flower.

One Step Further
What is your favorite flower? Draw a picture of a beautiful garden full of flowers.

Everyday Success First Grade

46 — Same and Different

Same and Different

Reading to find out how things are alike or different can help you picture and remember what you read. Things that are alike are called **similarities**. Things that are not alike are called **differences**.

Similarity: Beth and Michelle are both girls.
Difference: Beth has short hair, but Michelle has long hair.

Directions: Read the story.

Michelle and Beth are wearing new dresses. Both dresses are striped and have four shiny buttons. Each dress has a belt and a pocket. Beth's dress is blue and white, white Michelle's is yellow and white. The stripes on Beth's dress go up and down. Stripes on Michelle's dress go from side to side. Beth's pocket is bigger with room for a kitten.

Directions: Add the details. Color the dresses. Show how the dresses are alike and how they are different.

Beth's Dress **Michelle's Dress**

One Step Further
Sit with a friend. Make a list of your similarities and differences.

Everyday Success First Grade

47 — Comparing Cars

Same and Different

Directions: Read the story.

Sarah built a car for a race. Sarah's car has wheels, a steering wheel, and a place to sit just like the family car. It doesn't have a motor, a key, or a gas pedal. Sarah came in second in last year's race. This year, she hopes to win the race.

Directions: Write **S** beside the things Sarah's car has that are like things the family car has. Write **D** beside the things that are different.

S — steering wheel
D — motor
D — gas pedal
S — seat
S — wheels

One Step Further
Make a list of other things a family car would have.

Everyday Success First Grade

ANSWER KEY

BASIC SKILLS

48 — Color the Path

Directions: Color the path the girl should take to go home. Use the sentences to help you.

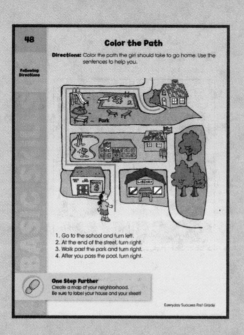

1. Go to the school and turn left.
2. At the end of the street, turn right.
3. Walk past the park and turn right.
4. After you pass the pool, turn right.

One Step Further
Create a map of your neighborhood. Be sure to label your house and your street!

Everyday Success First Grade

49 — Following Directions

Directions: Look at the pictures. Follow the directions in each box.

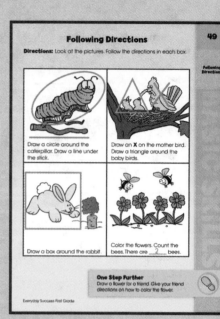

Draw a circle around the caterpillar. Draw a line under the stick.

Draw an **X** on the mother bird. Draw a triangle around the baby birds.

Draw a box around the rabbit.

Color the flowers. Count the bees. There are ___2___ bees.

One Step Further
Draw a flower for a friend. Give your friend directions on how to color the flower.

Everyday Success First Grade

50 — Fun With Directions

Directions: Follow the number code to color the balloons. Color the clown, too.

1 — blue   2 — orange   3 — yellow   4 — green   5 — purple
6 — brown   7 — red   8 — gray   9 — tan   10 — pink

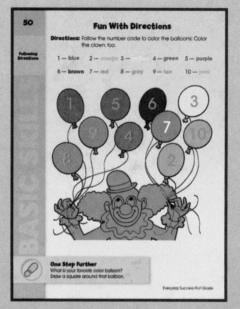

One Step Further
What is your favorite color balloon? Draw a square around that balloon.

Everyday Success First Grade

51 — Draw With Directions

Directions: Follow the directions to complete the picture.

1. Draw a smiling face on the sun.
2. Color the fish blue. Draw two more blue fish in the water.
3. Draw a **brown** bird under the cloud. Draw blue raindrops under the cloud.
4. Color the boat red. Color one sail pink. Color the other sail green.
5. Color the starfish orange. Draw two more orange starfish.

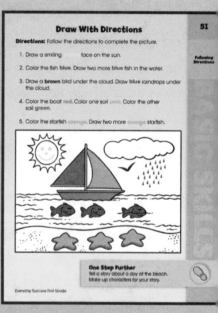

One Step Further
Tell a story about a day at the beach. Make up characters for your story.

Everyday Success First Grade

52 — Directions for Decorating

Directions: Follow the directions to decorate the bedroom.

Draw a red ▢ between the two 🩴🩴.

Draw a 🪑 under the window. Color it green.

Draw three big 🌸 on the wall. Color them orange.

Draw a picture of something you would like to have in your bedroom. Drawings will vary.

One Step Further
How is your room decorated? How would you like to decorate your room?

Everyday Success First Grade

53 — Following Directions

Read the sentences. Then, follow the directions.

Directions: Jared is making a snowman. He needs your help. Draw a **black** hat on the snowman. Draw red buttons. Now, draw a green scarf. Draw a happy face on the snowman.

One Step Further
What else would you see on a snowy winter day? Draw it in the picture.

Everyday Success First Grade

54

Following Directions

Follow the directions to make a paper sack puppet.

Directions: Find a small sack that fits your hand. Cut out teeth from colored paper. Glue them on the sack. Cut out ears. Glue them on the sack. Cut out eyes, a nose, and a tongue. Glue them all on.

Directions: Number the pictures **1, 2, 3,** and **4** to show the correct order.

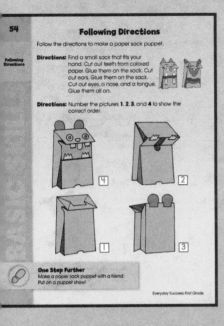

One Step Further
Make a paper sack puppet with a friend. Put on a puppet show!

Everyday Success First Grade

55

Draw a Tiger

Directions: Follow directions to complete the picture of the tiger.

1. Draw **black** stripes on the tiger's body and tail.
2. Color the tiger's tongue red.
3. Draw claws on the feet.
4. Draw a **black** nose and two **black** eyes on the tiger's face.
5. Color the rest of the tiger orange.
6. Draw tall, green grass for the tiger to sleep in.

One Step Further
What is your favorite animal?
What steps do you take to draw this animal?

Everyday Success First Grade

56

Color Names

Directions: Trace the letters to write the name of each color. Then, write the name again by yourself.

Example:

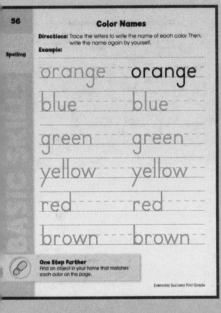

orange   orange

blue   blue

green   green

yellow   yellow

red   red

brown   brown

One Step Further
Find an object in your home that matches each color on the page.

Everyday Success First Grade

57

Color Names: Sentences

Directions: Use the color words to complete these sentences. Then, put a period at the end.

Example: My new [mittens] are **orange.**

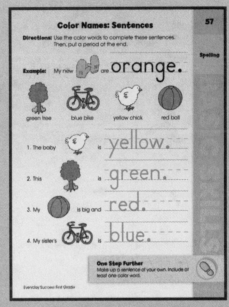

green tree   blue bike   yellow chick   red ball

1. The baby [chick] is **yellow.**

2. This [tree] is **green.**

3. My [ball] is big and **red.**

4. My sister's [bike] is **blue.**

One Step Further
Make up a sentence of your own. Include at least one color word.

Everyday Success First Grade

58

Animal Names

Directions: Fill in the missing letters for each word.

Example:

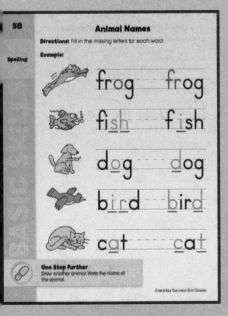

frog   frog

f**i**sh   f**i**sh

d**o**g   d**o**g

b**ir**d   b**ir**d

c**a**t   c**a**t

One Step Further
Draw another animal. Write the name of the animal.

Everyday Success First Grade

59

Animal Names: Sentences

A **sentence** tells about something.

Directions: These sentences tell about animals. Write the word that completes each sentence.

Example:

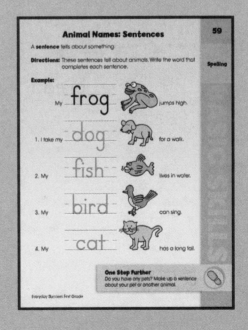

My **frog** jumps high.

1. I take my **dog** for a walk.

2. My **fish** lives in water.

3. My **bird** can sing.

4. My **cat** has a long tail.

One Step Further
Do you have any pets? Make up a sentence about your pet or another animal.

Everyday Success First Grade

ANSWER KEY

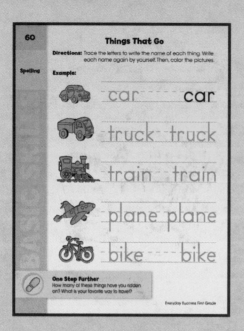

60 · Spelling

Things That Go

Directions: Trace the letters to write the name of each thing. Write each name again by yourself. Then, color the pictures.

Example:

car · car

truck · truck

train · train

plane · plane

bike · bike

One Step Further
How many of these things have you ridden on? What is your favorite way to travel?

Everyday Success First Grade

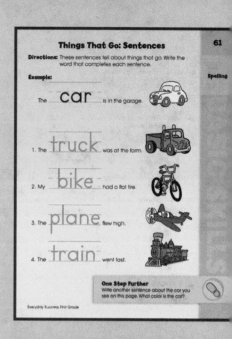

Things That Go: Sentences

61 · Spelling

Directions: These sentences tell about things that go. Write the word that completes each sentence.

Example:

The __car__ is in the garage.

1. The __truck__ was at the farm.

2. My __bike__ had a flat tire.

3. The __plane__ flew high.

4. The __train__ went fast.

One Step Further
Write another sentence about the car you see on this page. What color is the car?

Everyday Success First Grade

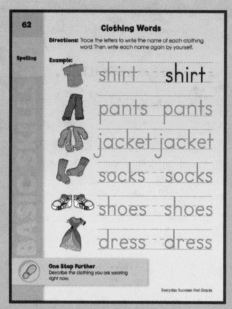

62 · Spelling

Clothing Words

Directions: Trace the letters to write the name of each clothing word. Then, write each name again by yourself.

Example:

shirt · shirt

pants · pants

jacket · jacket

socks · socks

shoes · shoes

dress · dress

One Step Further
Describe the clothing you are wearing right now.

Everyday Success First Grade

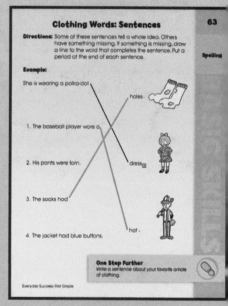

Clothing Words: Sentences

63 · Spelling

Directions: Some of these sentences tell a whole idea. Others have something missing. If something is missing, draw a line to the word that completes the sentence. Put a period at the end of each sentence.

Example:

She is wearing a polka-dot ___

holes.

1. The baseball player wore a ___

dress.

2. His pants were torn.

hat.

3. The socks had ___

4. The jacket had blue buttons.

One Step Further
Write a sentence about your favorite article of clothing.

Everyday Success First Grade

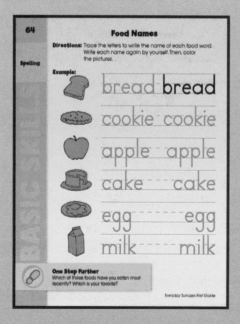

64 · Spelling

Food Names

Directions: Trace the letters to write the name of each food word. Write each name again by yourself. Then, color the pictures.

Example:

bread · bread

cookie · cookie

apple · apple

cake · cake

egg · egg

milk · milk

One Step Further
Which of these foods have you eaten most recently? Which is your favorite?

Everyday Success First Grade

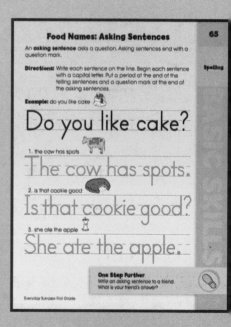

Food Names: Asking Sentences

65 · Spelling

An **asking sentence** asks a question. Asking sentences end with a question mark.

Directions: Write each sentence on the line. Begin each sentence with a capital letter. Put a period at the end of the telling sentences and a question mark at the end of the asking sentences.

Example: do you like cake

Do you like cake?

1. the cow has spots

The cow has spots.

2. is that cookie good

Is that cookie good?

3. she ate the apple

She ate the apple.

One Step Further
Write an asking sentence to a friend. What is your friend's answer?

Everyday Success First Grade

66 — Number Words

Spelling

Directions: Trace the letters to write the name of each number. Then, color the number pictures.

1 one   2 two

3 three   4 four

5 five   6 six

7 seven   8 eight

9 nine   10 ten

One Step Further
How old are you? Circle that number.
Draw a birthday cake with candles.

Everyday Success First Grade

67 — Number Words: Asking Sentences

Spelling

Directions: Use a number word to answer each question.

| one | five | seven | three | eight |

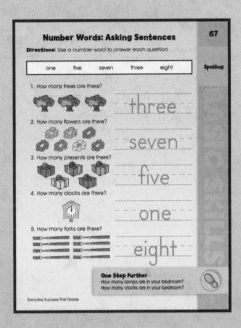

1. How many trees are there?   three

2. How many flowers are there?   seven

3. How many presents are there?   five

4. How many clocks are there?   one

5. How many forks are there?   eight

One Step Further
How many lamps are in your bedroom?
How many clocks are in your bedroom?

Everyday Success First Grade

68 — Action Words

Spelling

Action words tell things we can do.

Directions: Trace the letters to write each action word. Then, write the action word again by yourself.

Example:

sleep   sleep

run   run

make   make

ride   ride

play   play

stop   stop

One Step Further
What other action words can you think of?
Do those actions.

Everyday Success First Grade

69 — Action Words: More Than One

Spelling

To show more than one of something, add **s** to the end of the word.

Example: one cat   two cats

Directions: In each sentence, add **s** to show more than one. Then, write the action word that completes each sentence.

Example:

The frog   s   sleep   in the sun.

| sit | jump | stop | ride |

1. The boy   s   sit   on the fence.

2. The car   s   stop   at the sign.

3. The girl   s   jump   in the water.

4. The dog   s   ride   in the wagon.

One Step Further
Think of a friend. Write a sentence about
something you and your friend do together.

Everyday Success First Grade

70 — Action Words: Asking Sentences

Spelling

Directions: Write an asking sentence about each picture. Begin each sentence with **can**. Add an action word. Begin each asking sentence with a capital letter and end it with a question mark.

Example: I with you can

Can I sit with you?

1. she can

Can she cook?

2. with you can I

Can I play with you?

3. can she fast

Can she run fast?

One Step Further
How fast can you run?
Ask an adult to time you.

Everyday Success First Grade

71 — Sense Words

Spelling

Directions: Circle the word that is spelled correctly. Then, write the correct spelling in the blank.

Example:

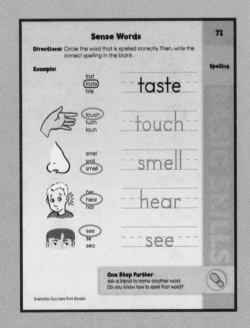

tast / (taste) / tste   taste

touch / tuch / touh   touch

smel / smil / (smell)   smell

har / (hear) / hair   hear

(see) / se / sea   see

One Step Further
Ask a friend to name another word.
Do you know how to spell that word?

Everyday Success First Grade

ANSWER KEY

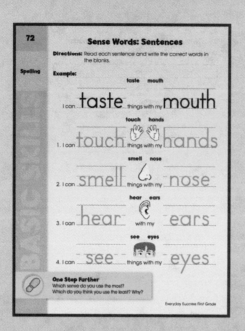

72 Spelling

Sense Words: Sentences

Directions: Read each sentence and write the correct words in the blanks.

Example:

taste   mouth

I can **taste** things with my **mouth**

touch   hands

1. I can **touch** things with my **hands**

smell   nose

2. I can **smell** things with my **nose**

hear   ears

3. I can **hear** with my **ears**

see   eyes

4. I can **see** things with my **eyes**

One Step Further
Which sense do you use the most?
Which do you think you use the least? Why?

Everyday Success First Grade

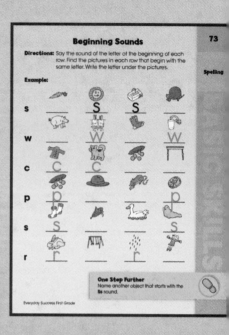

Beginning Sounds   **73** Spelling

Directions: Say the sound of the letter at the beginning of each row. Find the pictures in each row that begin with the same letter. Write the letter under the pictures.

Example:

s   S   S

w   W   W

c   C   C

p   p   p

s   S   S

r   r   r

One Step Further
Name another object that starts with the **Ss** sound.

Everyday Success First Grade

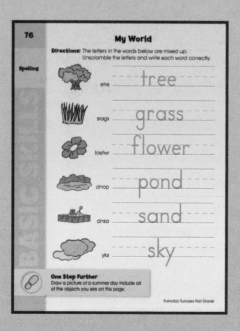

74 Spelling

Weather Words: Sentences

Directions: Write the weather word that completes each sentence. Put a period at the end of the telling sentences and a question mark at the end of the asking sentences.

Example:

Do flowers grow in the **sun ?**

| rain | water | wet | hot |

1. The sun makes me **hot.**

2. When it rains, the grass gets **wet.**

3. Do you think it will **rain** on our picnic **?**

4. Should you drink the **water** from the rain **?**

One Step Further
What is the weather like right now?
Write a sentence about it.

Everyday Success First Grade

My World   **75** Spelling

Directions: Fill in the missing letters for each word.

tree   tree
grass   grass
flower   flower
pond   pond
sand   sand
sky   sky

One Step Further
Look outside. How many of the objects on this page can you see?

Everyday Success First Grade

76 Spelling

My World

Directions: The letters in the words below are mixed up. Unscramble the letters and write each word correctly.

etre   **tree**

srags   **grass**

loetwr   **flower**

dnop   **pond**

dnsa   **sand**

yka   **sky**

One Step Further
Draw a picture of a summer day. Include all of the objects you see on this page.

Everyday Success First Grade

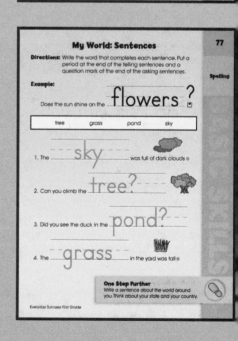

My World: Sentences   **77** Spelling

Directions: Write the word that completes each sentence. Put a period at the end of the telling sentences and a question mark at the end of the asking sentences.

Example:

Does the sun shine on the **flowers ?**

| tree | grass | pond | sky |

1. The **sky** was full of dark clouds **.**

2. Can you climb the **tree?**

3. Did you see the duck in the **pond?**

4. The **grass** in the yard was tall **.**

One Step Further
Write a sentence about the world around you. Think about your state and your country.

Everyday Success First Grade

Everyday Success First Grade

The Parts of My Body: Sentences

78

Spelling

Directions: Write the word that completes each sentence. Put a period at the end of the telling sentences and a question mark at the end of the asking sentences.

Example:

I wear my hat on my __head__ .

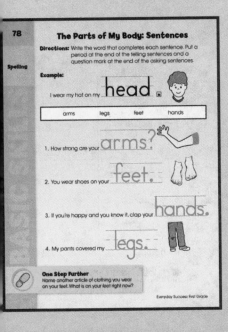

arms	legs	feet	hands

1. How strong are your __arms?__
2. You wear shoes on your __feet.__
3. If you're happy and you know it, clap your __hands.__
4. My pants covered my __legs.__

One Step Further
Name another article of clothing you wear on your feet. What is on your feet right now?

Everyday Success First Grade

The Parts of My Body: Sentences

79

Spelling

Directions: Read the sentence parts below. Draw a line from the first part of the sentence to the second part that completes it.

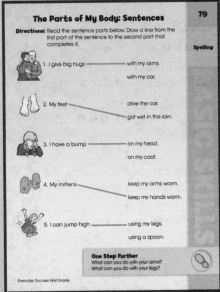

1. I give big hugs — with my arms.
   with my ear.
2. My feet — drive the car.
   got wet in the rain.
3. I have a bump — on my head.
   on my coat.
4. My mittens — keep my arms warm.
   keep my hands warm.
5. I can jump high — using my legs.
   using a spoon.

One Step Further
What can you do with your arms?
What can you do with your legs?

Everyday Success First Grade

The Parts of My Body: Sentences

80

Spelling

Directions: Read the two sentences on each line and draw a line between them. Then, write each sentence again on the lines below. Begin each sentence with a capital letter, and end each one with a period or a question mark.

Example: wash your hands | they are dirty

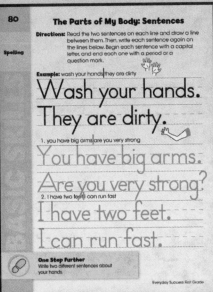

Wash your hands.
They are dirty.

1. you have big arms | are you very strong

You have big arms.
Are you very strong?

2. I have two feet | I can run fast

I have two feet.
I can run fast.

One Step Further
Write two different sentences about your hands.

Everyday Success First Grade

Addition

82

Addition

Putting numbers together is called **addition**. When you add two numbers together, you get a **total**, or **sum**. The symbol used for addition is called a **plus sign (+)**. The symbol used for a total is an **equal sign (=)**.

Directions: Follow the instructions below to create and solve the addition problems.

One pony is eating hay.

Draw one more pony in this box.

Write the total number of ponies.

+ [Drawings will vary.] = 2

One lamb is jumping.

Draw two more lambs in this box.

Write the total number of lambs.

+ [Drawings will vary.] = 3

One Step Further
Pretend you own one book. You are given two more books. How many do you have now?

Everyday Success First Grade

Addition

83

Addition

Directions: Count the shapes and write the numbers below to tell how many in all.

1 + 1 = 2

2 + 1 = 3

1 + 2 = 3

3 + 1 = 4

One Step Further
How many square objects can you find in your bedroom? Count them.

Everyday Success First Grade

Sums 0 to 3

84

Addition

Directions: Add.

$1 + 1 = 2$

$\begin{array}{r} 1 \\ +1 \\ \hline 2 \end{array}$

$2 + 1 = 3$

$\begin{array}{r} 2 \\ +1 \\ \hline 3 \end{array}$

$1 + 2 = 3$

$\begin{array}{r} 1 \\ +2 \\ \hline 3 \end{array}$

$2 + 0 = 2$

$\begin{array}{r} 2 \\ +0 \\ \hline 2 \end{array}$

$3 + 0 = 3$

$\begin{array}{r} 3 \\ +0 \\ \hline 3 \end{array}$

$0 + 2 = 2$

$\begin{array}{r} 0 \\ +2 \\ \hline 2 \end{array}$

$0 + 3 = 3$

$\begin{array}{r} 0 \\ +3 \\ \hline 3 \end{array}$

$0 + 0 = 0$

$\begin{array}{r} 0 \\ +0 \\ \hline 0 \end{array}$

$1 + 0 = 1$

$\begin{array}{r} 1 \\ +0 \\ \hline 1 \end{array}$

$0 + 1 = 1$

$\begin{array}{r} 0 \\ +1 \\ \hline 1 \end{array}$

One Step Further
Find two pencils. Find one crayon. Add how many objects there are.

Everyday Success First Grade

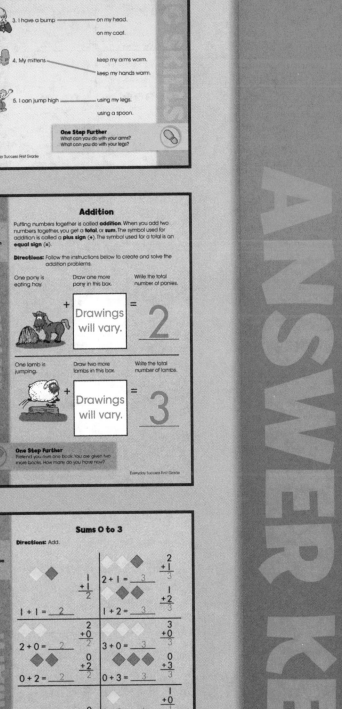
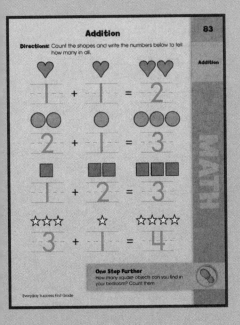

Sums of 4 and 5 — 85
Addition

Directions: Add.

$4 + 1 = \underline{5}$ $\begin{array}{r} 4 \\ +1 \\ \hline 5 \end{array}$ $2 + 3 = \underline{5}$ $\begin{array}{r} 2 \\ +3 \\ \hline 5 \end{array}$

$1 + 4 = \underline{5}$ $\begin{array}{r} 1 \\ +4 \\ \hline 5 \end{array}$ $3 + 2 = \underline{5}$ $\begin{array}{r} 3 \\ +2 \\ \hline 5 \end{array}$

$2 + 2 = \underline{4}$ $\begin{array}{r} 2 \\ +2 \\ \hline 4 \end{array}$ $4 + 0 = \underline{4}$ $\begin{array}{r} 4 \\ +0 \\ \hline 4 \end{array}$

$\quad$ $0 + 4 = \underline{4}$ $\begin{array}{r} 0 \\ +4 \\ \hline 4 \end{array}$

$5 + 0 = \underline{5}$ $\begin{array}{r} 5 \\ +0 \\ \hline 5 \end{array}$ $1 + 3 = \underline{4}$ $\begin{array}{r} 1 \\ +3 \\ \hline 4 \end{array}$

$0 + 5 = \underline{5}$ $\begin{array}{r} 0 \\ +5 \\ \hline 5 \end{array}$ $3 + 1 = \underline{4}$ $\begin{array}{r} 3 \\ +1 \\ \hline 4 \end{array}$

One Step Further
Find four buttons. Find one shell. Add how many objects there are.

Everyday Success First Grade

Sums of 6 — 86
Addition

Directions: Add.

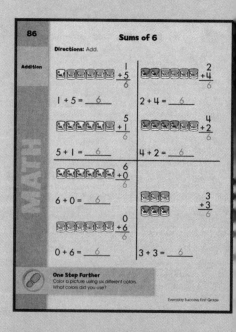

$1 + 5 = \underline{6}$ $\begin{array}{r} 1 \\ +5 \\ \hline 6 \end{array}$ $2 + 4 = \underline{6}$ $\begin{array}{r} 2 \\ +4 \\ \hline 6 \end{array}$

$5 + 1 = \underline{6}$ $\begin{array}{r} 5 \\ +1 \\ \hline 6 \end{array}$ $4 + 2 = \underline{6}$ $\begin{array}{r} 4 \\ +2 \\ \hline 6 \end{array}$

$6 + 0 = \underline{6}$ $\begin{array}{r} 6 \\ +0 \\ \hline 6 \end{array}$ $3 + 3 = \underline{6}$ $\begin{array}{r} 3 \\ +3 \\ \hline 6 \end{array}$

$0 + 6 = \underline{6}$ $\begin{array}{r} 0 \\ +6 \\ \hline 6 \end{array}$

One Step Further
Color a picture using six different colors. What colors did you use?

Everyday Success First Grade

Sums of 7 — 87
Addition

Directions: Add.

$3 + 4 = \underline{7}$ $\begin{array}{r} 3 \\ +4 \\ \hline 7 \end{array}$ $6 + 1 = \underline{7}$ $\begin{array}{r} 6 \\ +1 \\ \hline 7 \end{array}$

$4 + 3 = \underline{7}$ $\begin{array}{r} 4 \\ +3 \\ \hline 7 \end{array}$ $1 + 6 = \underline{7}$ $\begin{array}{r} 1 \\ +6 \\ \hline 7 \end{array}$

$7 + 0 = \underline{7}$ $\begin{array}{r} 7 \\ +0 \\ \hline 7 \end{array}$ $2 + 5 = \underline{7}$ $\begin{array}{r} 2 \\ +5 \\ \hline 7 \end{array}$

$0 + 7 = \underline{7}$ $\begin{array}{r} 0 \\ +7 \\ \hline 7 \end{array}$ $5 + 2 = \underline{7}$ $\begin{array}{r} 5 \\ +2 \\ \hline 7 \end{array}$

One Step Further
Roll a die seven times. What numbers did you roll?

Everyday Success First Grade

Sums of 8 — 88
Addition

Directions: Add.

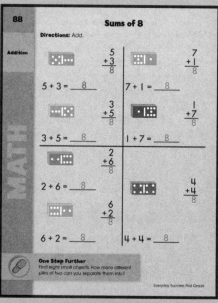

$5 + 3 = \underline{8}$ $\begin{array}{r} 5 \\ +3 \\ \hline 8 \end{array}$ $7 + 1 = \underline{8}$ $\begin{array}{r} 7 \\ +1 \\ \hline 8 \end{array}$

$3 + 5 = \underline{8}$ $\begin{array}{r} 3 \\ +5 \\ \hline 8 \end{array}$ $1 + 7 = \underline{8}$ $\begin{array}{r} 1 \\ +7 \\ \hline 8 \end{array}$

$2 + 6 = \underline{8}$ $\begin{array}{r} 2 \\ +6 \\ \hline 8 \end{array}$ $\begin{array}{r} 4 \\ +4 \\ \hline 8 \end{array}$

$6 + 2 = \underline{8}$ $\begin{array}{r} 6 \\ +2 \\ \hline 8 \end{array}$ $4 + 4 = \underline{8}$

One Step Further
Find eight small objects. How many different piles of two can you separate them into?

Everyday Success First Grade

Sums of 9 — 89
Addition

Directions: Add.

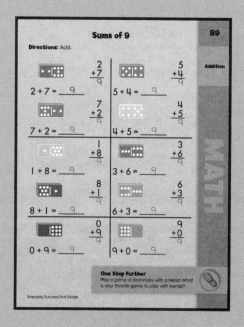

$2 + 7 = \underline{9}$ $\begin{array}{r} 2 \\ +7 \\ \hline 9 \end{array}$ $5 + 4 = \underline{9}$ $\begin{array}{r} 5 \\ +4 \\ \hline 9 \end{array}$

$7 + 2 = \underline{9}$ $\begin{array}{r} 7 \\ +2 \\ \hline 9 \end{array}$ $4 + 5 = \underline{9}$ $\begin{array}{r} 4 \\ +5 \\ \hline 9 \end{array}$

$1 + 8 = \underline{9}$ $\begin{array}{r} 1 \\ +8 \\ \hline 9 \end{array}$ $3 + 6 = \underline{9}$ $\begin{array}{r} 3 \\ +6 \\ \hline 9 \end{array}$

$8 + 1 = \underline{9}$ $\begin{array}{r} 8 \\ +1 \\ \hline 9 \end{array}$ $6 + 3 = \underline{9}$ $\begin{array}{r} 6 \\ +3 \\ \hline 9 \end{array}$

$0 + 9 = \underline{9}$ $\begin{array}{r} 0 \\ +9 \\ \hline 9 \end{array}$ $9 + 0 = \underline{9}$ $\begin{array}{r} 9 \\ +0 \\ \hline 9 \end{array}$

One Step Further
Play a game of dominoes with a friend. What is your favorite game to play with friends?

Everyday Success First Grade

Sums of 10 — 90
Addition

Directions: Add.

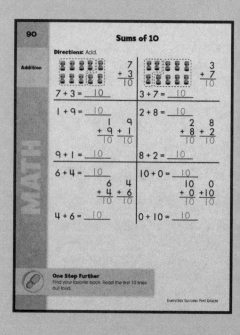

$7 + 3 = \underline{10}$ $\begin{array}{r} 7 \\ +3 \\ \hline 10 \end{array}$ $3 + 7 = \underline{10}$ $\begin{array}{r} 3 \\ +7 \\ \hline 10 \end{array}$

$1 + 9 = \underline{10}$ $2 + 8 = \underline{10}$

$9 + 1 = \underline{10}$ $\begin{array}{r} 1 \\ +9 \\ \hline 10 \end{array} \begin{array}{r} 9 \\ +1 \\ \hline 10 \end{array}$ $8 + 2 = \underline{10}$ $\begin{array}{r} 2 \\ +8 \\ \hline 10 \end{array} \begin{array}{r} 8 \\ +2 \\ \hline 10 \end{array}$

$6 + 4 = \underline{10}$ $10 + 0 = \underline{10}$

$4 + 6 = \underline{10}$ $\begin{array}{r} 6 \\ +4 \\ \hline 10 \end{array} \begin{array}{r} 4 \\ +6 \\ \hline 10 \end{array}$ $0 + 10 = \underline{10}$ $\begin{array}{r} 10 \\ +0 \\ \hline 10 \end{array} \begin{array}{r} 0 \\ +10 \\ \hline 10 \end{array}$

One Step Further
Find your favorite book. Read the first 10 lines out loud.

Everyday Success First Grade

Addition 1, 2
91

Addition

Directions: Count the cats and tell how many.

+ = **2**

+ = **3**

+ = **4**

One Step Further
Add the number of cats you have to the number of cats your friend has.

Everyday Success First Grade

92

Addition

Addition 3, 4, 5, 6

Directions: Practice writing the numbers and then add. Draw dots to help, if needed.

3 3 3 3   2   1
4 4 4 4   +4   +4
5 5 5 5   6   5
6 6 6 6

3   1
+2   +2
5   3

One Step Further
Count the pillows on your bed. Then, count the blankets. Add them together.

Everyday Success First Grade

Addition 7, 8, 9
93

Addition

Directions: Practice writing the numbers and then add. Draw dots to help, if needed.

7 7 7 7   8   3
8 8 8 8   +1   +5
9 9 9 9   9   8

2   6
+7   +1
9   7

One Step Further
Divide your crayons into two piles. Count the crayons and add each group together.

Everyday Success First Grade

94

Addition

Addition

The Barton family is having a picnic. But the ants have carried away their food.

Directions: Use an addition equation to find out how many ants took food. The first one is done for you.

How many ants carried away fruit?   1 + 2 = 3

How many ants carried away vegetables?   2 + 3 = 5

How many ants carried away hot dogs?   3 + 3 = 6

How many ants carried away bread?   5 + 2 = 7

One Step Further
Have a picnic with your family. What foods do you eat?

Everyday Success First Grade

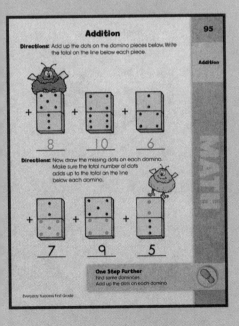

Addition
95

Addition

Directions: Add up the dots on the domino pieces below. Write the total on the line below each piece.

+ ____ + ____ + ____

8   10   6

Directions: Now, draw the missing dots on each domino. Make sure the total number of dots adds up to the total on the line below each domino.

+ ____ + ____ + ____

7   9   5

One Step Further
Find some dominoes. Add up the dots on each domino.

Everyday Success First Grade

96

Addition
Story
Problems

Addition

Mrs. Murky asked three monster girls and two monster boys to come to the front of the class. She said, "If I have three monster girls and I add two monster boys, how many monster children do I have all together?"

Directions: Now, do the same problem on the board, but count the two boys first.

3 + 2 = 5
2 + 3 = 5

Does it matter which group is counted first? ____ no

One Step Further
How many girls are in your class at school? How many boys?

Everyday Success First Grade

Everyday Success First Grade

Problem Solving — 97

Directions: Solve each problem.

There are five white 🦋.
There are four blue 🦋.
How many in all?

$$\begin{array}{r} 5 \\ +4 \\ \hline 9 \end{array}$$

There are three 🐑.
Seven more 🐑 come.
How many are there now?

$$\begin{array}{r} 3 \\ +7 \\ \hline 10 \end{array}$$

Beth has nine.
She buys one more.
Now how many does she have?

$$\begin{array}{r} 9 \\ +1 \\ \hline 10 \end{array}$$

There are six.
There are three.
How many in all?

$$\begin{array}{r} 6 \\ +3 \\ \hline 9 \end{array}$$

There were eight 🐕.
Two more come.
Then how many were there?

$$\begin{array}{r} 8 \\ +2 \\ \hline 10 \end{array}$$

Addition Story Problems

One Step Further
How many T-shirts do you own? How many would you own if you bought one more?

Everyday Success First Grade

Plenty to Wear! — 98

Directions: The key words "in all" tell you to add. Circle the key words "in all" and solve the problems.

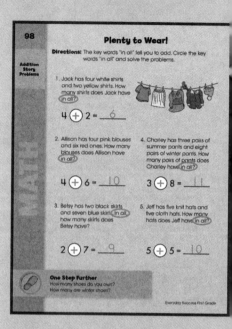

1. Jack has four white shirts and two yellow shirts. How many shirts does Jack have (in all)?

$$4 \oplus 2 = \underline{6}$$

2. Allison has four pink blouses and six red ones. How many blouses does Allison have (in all)?

$$4 \oplus 6 = \underline{10}$$

3. Betsy has two black skirts and seven blue skirts. (In all) how many skirts does Betsy have?

$$2 \oplus 7 = \underline{9}$$

4. Charley has three pairs of summer pants and eight pairs of winter pants. How many pairs of pants does Charley have (in all)?

$$3 \oplus 8 = \underline{11}$$

5. Jeff has five knit hats and five cloth hats. How many hats does Jeff have (in all)?

$$5 \oplus 5 = \underline{10}$$

Addition Story Problems

One Step Further
How many shoes do you own?
How many are winter shoes?

Everyday Success First Grade

Problems in the Park — 99

Directions: Circle the addition key words "in all." Write a number sentence to solve each problem.

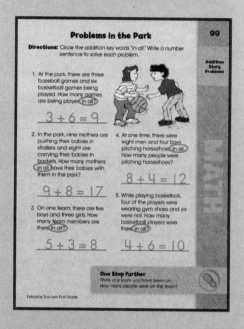

1. At the park, there are three baseball games and six basketball games being played. How many games are being played (in all)?

$$3 + 6 = 9$$

2. In the park, nine mothers are pushing their babies in strollers and eight are carrying their babies in baskets. How many mothers (in all) have their babies with them in the park?

$$9 + 8 = 17$$

3. On one team, there are five boys and three girls. How many team members are there (in all)?

$$5 + 3 = 8$$

4. At one time, there were eight men and four boys pitching horseshoes. (In all) how many people were pitching horseshoes?

$$8 + 4 = 12$$

5. While playing basketball, four of the players were wearing gym shoes and six were not. How many basketball players were there (in all)?

$$4 + 6 = 10$$

Addition Story Problems

One Step Further
Think of a team you have been on. How many people were on the team?

Everyday Success First Grade

Additional Story Problems — 100

Directions: Circle the addition key words "in all." Write a number sentence to solve each problem.

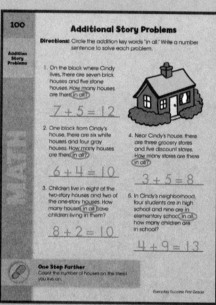

1. On the block where Cindy lives, there are seven brick houses and five stone houses. How many houses are there (in all)?

$$7 + 5 = 12$$

2. One block from Cindy's house, there are six white houses and four gray houses. How many houses are there (in all)?

$$6 + 4 = 10$$

3. Children live in eight of the two-story houses and two of the one-story houses. How many houses (in all) have children living in them?

$$8 + 2 = 10$$

4. Near Cindy's house, there are three grocery stores and five discount stores. How many stores are there (in all)?

$$3 + 5 = 8$$

5. In Cindy's neighborhood, four students are in high school and nine are in elementary school. (In all) how many children are in school?

$$4 + 9 = 13$$

Addition Story Problems

One Step Further
Count the number of houses on the street you live on.

Everyday Success First Grade

Solving Stories — 101

Directions: Write a number sentence to solve each problem.

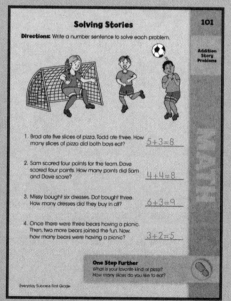

1. Brad ate five slices of pizza. Todd ate three. How many slices of pizza did both boys eat?

$$5 + 3 = 8$$

2. Sam scored four points for the team. Dave scored four points. How many points did Sam and Dave score?

$$4 + 4 = 8$$

3. Missy bought six dresses. Dot bought three. How many dresses did they buy in all?

$$6 + 3 = 9$$

4. Once there were three bears having a picnic. Then, two more bears joined the fun. Now how many bears were having a picnic?

$$3 + 2 = 5$$

Addition Story Problems

One Step Further
What is your favorite kind of pizza? How many slices do you like to eat?

Everyday Success First Grade

Beary Good — 102

Directions: Put counters on each bear to add. Write the sums below.

$$\begin{array}{r} 6 \\ +1 \\ \hline 7 \end{array} \quad \begin{array}{r} 3 \\ +4 \\ \hline 7 \end{array} \quad \begin{array}{r} 2 \\ +3 \\ \hline 5 \end{array} \quad \begin{array}{r} 5 \\ +2 \\ \hline 7 \end{array} \quad \begin{array}{r} 7 \\ +1 \\ \hline 8 \end{array}$$

$$\begin{array}{r} 8 \\ +0 \\ \hline 8 \end{array} \quad \begin{array}{r} 4 \\ +5 \\ \hline 9 \end{array} \quad \begin{array}{r} 3 \\ +6 \\ \hline 9 \end{array} \quad \begin{array}{r} 2 \\ +6 \\ \hline 8 \end{array} \quad \begin{array}{r} 3 \\ +5 \\ \hline 8 \end{array}$$

Addition Practice

One Step Further
How many teddy bears do you own? Are teddy bears your favorite toy?

Everyday Success First Grade

Air Bear Addition

103

Addition Practice

Directions: Help Buddy off the ground. Add to find the sum. Then, color the clouds with sums of 9 to find the right path.

5 + 5 = 10   7 + 4 = 11   3 + 7 = 10
6 + 3 = 9   8 + 1 = 9   6 + 4 = 10
2 + 7 = 9   2 + 5 = 7   5 + 4 = 9   10 + 1 = 11
6 + 5 = 11   3 + 4 = 7   9 + 0 = 9   2 + 5 = 7
2 + 4 = 6   5 + 5 = 10   4 + 5 = 9   3 + 2 = 5
2 + 6 = 8   8 + 2 = 10   3 + 6 = 9

One Step Further
Look up in the sky. How many clouds can you see?

Everyday Success First Grade

Practicing Addition

104

Addition Practice

Directions: Add.

6 + 4 = 10	7 + 2 = 9	4 + 4 = 8	4 + 5 = 9	9 + 1 = 10
2 + 7 = 9	6 + 2 = 8	9 + 0 = 9	2 + 5 = 7	1 + 4 = 5
8 + 1 = 9	2 + 2 = 4	3 + 6 = 9	1 + 7 = 8	7 + 3 = 10
2 + 3 = 5	2 + 8 = 10	3 + 5 = 8	8 + 2 = 10	6 + 1 = 7
1 + 9 = 10	6 + 3 = 9	3 + 4 = 7	5 + 2 = 7	5 + 4 = 9

One Step Further
What two numbers add up to equal your age?

Everyday Success First Grade

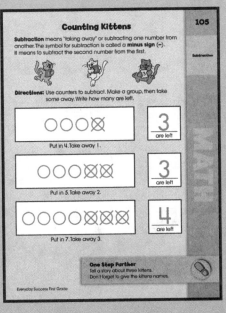

Counting Kittens

105

Subtraction

Subtraction means "taking away" or subtracting one number from another. The symbol for subtraction is called a **minus sign (−)**. It means to subtract the second number from the first.

Directions: Use counters to subtract. Make a group, then take some away. Write how many are left.

Put in 4. Take away 1.   **3** are left

Put in 5. Take away 2.   **3** are left

Put in 7. Take away 3.   **4** are left

One Step Further
Tell a story about three kittens. Don't forget to give the kittens names.

Everyday Success First Grade

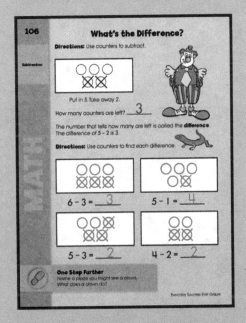

What's the Difference?

106

Subtraction

Directions: Use counters to subtract.

Put in 5. Take away 2.

How many counters are left? **3**

The number that tells how many are left is called the **difference**. The difference of 5 − 2 is 3.

Directions: Use counters to find each difference.

6 − 3 = **3**   5 − 1 = **4**
5 − 3 = **2**   4 − 2 = **2**

One Step Further
Name a place you might see a clown. What does a clown do?

Everyday Success First Grade

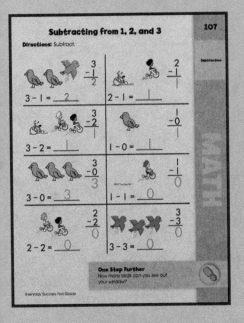

Subtracting from 1, 2, and 3

107

Subtraction

Directions: Subtract.

3 − 1 = 2   2 − 1 = 1
3 − 2 = 1   1 − 0 = 1
3 − 0 = 3   1 − 1 = 0
2 − 2 = 0   3 − 3 = 0

One Step Further
How many birds can you see out your window?

Everyday Success First Grade

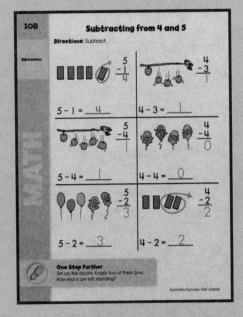

Subtracting from 4 and 5

108

Subtraction

Directions: Subtract.

5 − 1 = 4   4 − 3 = 1
5 − 4 = 1   4 − 4 = 0
5 − 2 = 3   4 − 2 = 2

One Step Further
Set up five blocks. Knock two of them over. How many are left standing?

Everyday Success First Grade

ANSWER KEY

Everyday Success First Grade

Subtracting from 6
Directions: Subtract.

$$\begin{array}{r} 6 \\ -1 \\ \hline 5 \end{array}$$

$$\begin{array}{r} 6 \\ -5 \\ \hline 1 \end{array}$$

6 - 1 = __5__   6 - 5 = __1__

$$\begin{array}{r} 6 \\ -4 \\ \hline 2 \end{array}$$

$$\begin{array}{r} 6 \\ -2 \\ \hline 4 \end{array}$$

6 - 4 = __2__   6 - 2 = __4__

$$\begin{array}{r} 6 \\ -3 \\ \hline 3 \end{array}$$

$$\begin{array}{r} 6 \\ -0 \\ \hline 6 \end{array}$$

6 - 3 = __3__   6 - 0 = __6__

One Step Further
Draw six flowers for the bees to land on.
Color each flower a different color.

Everyday Success First Grade

109 Subtraction

---

110 Subtraction

Subtracting from 7
Directions: Subtract.

$$\begin{array}{r} 7 \\ -6 \\ \hline 1 \end{array}$$

$$\begin{array}{r} 7 \\ -1 \\ \hline 6 \end{array}$$

7 - 6 = __1__   7 - 1 = __6__

$$\begin{array}{r} 7 \\ -3 \\ \hline 4 \end{array}$$

$$\begin{array}{r} 7 \\ -4 \\ \hline 3 \end{array}$$

7 - 3 = __4__   7 - 4 = __3__

$$\begin{array}{r} 7 \\ -7 \\ \hline 0 \end{array}$$

$$\begin{array}{r} 7 \\ -0 \\ \hline 7 \end{array}$$

7 - 7 = __0__   7 - 0 = __7__

$$\begin{array}{r} 7 \\ -2 \\ \hline 5 \end{array}$$

$$\begin{array}{r} 7 \\ -5 \\ \hline 2 \end{array}$$

7 - 2 = __5__   7 - 5 = __2__

One Step Further
Name the seven days of the week.
What day is your favorite?

Everyday Success First Grade

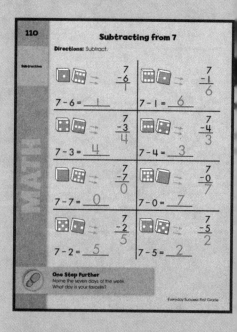

Subtracting from 8
Directions: Subtract.

$$\begin{array}{r} 8 \\ -7 \\ \hline 1 \end{array}$$

$$\begin{array}{r} 8 \\ -1 \\ \hline 7 \end{array}$$

8 - 7 = __1__   8 - 1 = __7__

$$\begin{array}{r} 8 \\ -2 \\ \hline 6 \end{array}$$

$$\begin{array}{r} 8 \\ -6 \\ \hline 2 \end{array}$$

8 - 2 = __6__   8 - 6 = __2__

$$\begin{array}{r} 8 \\ -4 \\ \hline 4 \end{array}$$

$$\begin{array}{r} 8 \\ -8 \\ \hline 0 \end{array}$$

8 - 4 = __4__   8 - 8 = __0__

$$\begin{array}{r} 8 \\ -3 \\ \hline 5 \end{array}$$

$$\begin{array}{r} 8 \\ -5 \\ \hline 3 \end{array}$$

8 - 3 = __5__   8 - 5 = __3__

One Step Further
Can you name at least eight states?
What state do you live in?

Everyday Success First Grade

111 Subtraction

---

112 Subtraction

Subtracting from 9
Directions: Subtract.

$$\begin{array}{r} 9 \\ -6 \\ \hline 3 \end{array}$$

$$\begin{array}{r} 9 \\ -3 \\ \hline 6 \end{array}$$

9 - 6 = __3__   9 - 3 = __6__

$$\begin{array}{r} 9 \\ -0 \\ \hline 9 \end{array}$$

$$\begin{array}{r} 9 \\ -9 \\ \hline 0 \end{array}$$

9 - 0 = __9__   9 - 9 = __0__

$$\begin{array}{r} 9 \\ -5 \\ \hline 4 \end{array}$$

$$\begin{array}{r} 9 \\ -4 \\ \hline 5 \end{array}$$

9 - 5 = __4__   9 - 4 = __5__

$$\begin{array}{r} 9 \\ -8 \\ \hline 1 \end{array}$$

$$\begin{array}{r} 9 \\ -1 \\ \hline 8 \end{array}$$

9 - 8 = __1__   9 - 1 = __8__

One Step Further
Roll two dice. How many rolls do you make
until you roll a total of nine?

Everyday Success First Grade

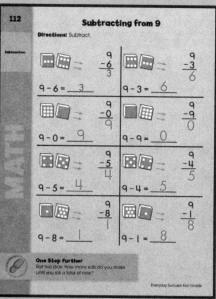

Subtracting from 10
Directions: Subtract.

$$\begin{array}{r} 10 \\ -1 \\ \hline 9 \end{array}$$

$$\begin{array}{r} 10 \\ -9 \\ \hline 1 \end{array}$$

10 - 1 = __9__   10 - 9 = __1__

10 - 7 = __3__   10 - 4 = __6__

$$\begin{array}{r} 10 \\ -7 \\ \hline 3 \end{array} \quad \begin{array}{r} 10 \\ -3 \\ \hline 7 \end{array}$$

$$\begin{array}{r} 10 \\ -4 \\ \hline 6 \end{array} \quad \begin{array}{r} 10 \\ -6 \\ \hline 4 \end{array}$$

10 - 3 = __7__   10 - 6 = __4__

10 - 8 = __2__

$$\begin{array}{r} 10 \\ -8 \\ \hline 2 \end{array} \quad \begin{array}{r} 10 \\ -2 \\ \hline 8 \end{array}$$

$$\begin{array}{r} 10 \\ -0 \\ \hline 10 \end{array}$$

10 - 2 = __8__   10 - 0 = __10__

One Step Further
Can you whistle? Try to whistle for 10 seconds
while standing on one foot.

Everyday Success First Grade

113 Subtraction

---

114 Subtraction

Subtraction 1, 2, 3
Directions: Practice writing the numbers and then subtract. Draw dots and cross them out, if needed.

1 | | |

2 2 2 2

3 3 3 3

$$\begin{array}{r} 3 \\ -1 \\ \hline 2 \end{array} \quad \begin{array}{r} 4 \\ -3 \\ \hline 1 \end{array}$$

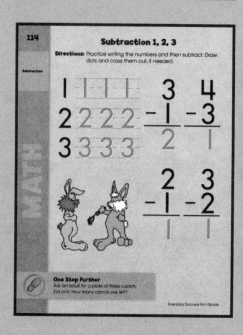

$$\begin{array}{r} 2 \\ -1 \\ \hline 1 \end{array} \quad \begin{array}{r} 3 \\ -2 \\ \hline 1 \end{array}$$

One Step Further
Ask an adult for a plate of three carrots.
Eat one. How many carrots are left?

Everyday Success First Grade

Everyday Success First Grade

Subtraction 4, 5, 6

115

Directions: Practice writing the numbers and then subtract. Draw dots and cross them out, if needed.

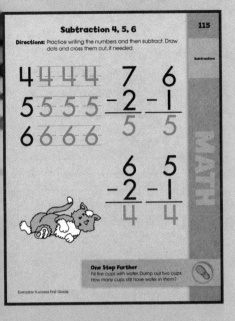

$$4\ 4\ 4\ 4$$
$$5\ 5\ 5\ 5$$
$$6\ 6\ 6\ 6$$

$$\begin{array}{r} 7 \\ -2 \\ \hline 5 \end{array}$$
$$\begin{array}{r} 6 \\ -1 \\ \hline 5 \end{array}$$

$$\begin{array}{r} 6 \\ -2 \\ \hline 4 \end{array}$$
$$\begin{array}{r} 5 \\ -1 \\ \hline 4 \end{array}$$

One Step Further
Fill five cups with water. Dump out two cups. How many cups still have water in them?

Everyday Success First Grade

116

Nutty Subtraction

Directions: Count the nuts in each dish. Write the answer on the line by each dish. Circle each problem with the same answer.

$$3$$
4 - 1 = 3
5 - 2 = 3

$$1$$
5 - 4 = 1
3 - 2 = 1

$$4$$
4 - 0 = 4
5 - 1 = 4

$$5$$
5 - 0 = 5
7 - 2 = 5

$$2$$
4 - 1
5 - 3
4 - 2 = 2

One Step Further
Find five peanuts or other small objects. Take away two. How many are left?

Everyday Success First Grade

Subtracting

117

Six silly green frogs were sitting on six lily pads.

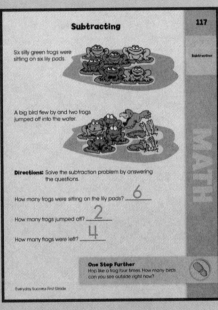

A big bird flew by and two frogs jumped off into the water.

Directions: Solve the subtraction problem by answering the questions.

How many frogs were sitting on the lily pads? 6

How many frogs jumped off? 2

How many frogs were left? 4

One Step Further
Hop like a frog four times. How many birds can you see outside right now?

Everyday Success First Grade

118

Subtracting

Four hungry cats went on a picnic.

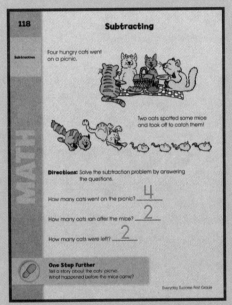

Two cats spotted some mice and took off to catch them!

Directions: Solve the subtraction problem by answering the questions.

How many cats went on the picnic? 4

How many cats ran after the mice? 2

How many cats were left? 2

One Step Further
Tell a story about the cats' picnic. What happened before the mice came?

Everyday Success First Grade

How Many Animals Are Left?

119

Directions: The key word "left" tells you to subtract. Circle the key word "left." Write a number sentence to solve each subtraction problem.

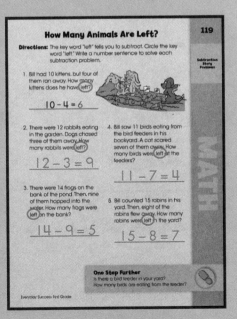

1. Bill had 10 kittens, but four of them ran away. How many kittens does he have left?

$$10 - 4 = 6$$

2. There were 12 rabbits eating in the garden. Dogs chased three of them away. How many rabbits were left?

$$12 - 3 = 9$$

3. There were 14 frogs on the bank of the pond. Then, nine of them hopped into the water. How many frogs were left on the bank?

$$14 - 9 = 5$$

4. Bill saw 11 birds eating from the bird feeders in his backyard. A cat scared seven of them away. How many birds were left at the feeders?

$$11 - 7 = 4$$

5. Bill counted 15 robins in his yard. Then, eight of the robins flew away. How many robins were left in the yard?

$$15 - 8 = 7$$

One Step Further
Is there a bird feeder in your yard? How many birds are eating from the feeder?

Everyday Success First Grade

120

How Many Left?

Directions: Solve each problem.

There are 10 white.
There are four blue.
How many more white than blue are there? 6

$$\begin{array}{r} 10 \\ -4 \\ \hline 6 \end{array}$$

Ten are on the table.
Two are broken.
How many are not broken? 8

$$\begin{array}{r} 10 \\ -2 \\ \hline 8 \end{array}$$

There are nine.
Six swim away.
How many are left? 3

$$\begin{array}{r} 9 \\ -6 \\ \hline 3 \end{array}$$

Joni wants nine.
She has five.
How many more does she need? 4

$$\begin{array}{r} 9 \\ -5 \\ \hline 4 \end{array}$$

There were 10.
Five melted.
How many did not melt? 5

$$\begin{array}{r} 10 \\ -5 \\ \hline 5 \end{array}$$

One Step Further
What color flowers are outside your home? Draw a picture of your favorite flower.

Everyday Success First Grade

ANSWER KEY

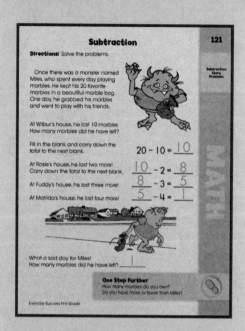

Subtraction 121

Directions: Solve the problems.

Once there was a monster named Miles, who spent every day playing marbles. He kept his 20 favorite marbles in a beautiful marble bag. One day, he grabbed his marbles and went to play with his friends.

At Wilbur's house, he lost 10 marbles. How many marbles did he have left?

Fill in the blank and carry down the total to the next blank.

$20 - 10 = \underline{10}$

At Rosie's house, he lost two more! Carry down the total to the next blank.

$\underline{10} - 2 = \underline{8}$

$\underline{8} - 3 = \underline{5}$

At Fuddy's house, he lost three more!

At Matilda's house, he lost four more!

$\underline{5} - 4 = \underline{1}$

What a sad day for Miles! How many marbles did he have left? $\underline{1}$

One Step Further
How many marbles do you own? Do you have more or fewer than Miles?

Everyday Success First Grade

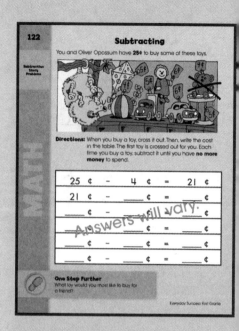

Subtracting 122

You and Oliver Opossum have 25¢ to buy some of these toys.

Directions: When you buy a toy, cross it out. Then, write the cost in the table. The first toy is crossed out for you. Each time you buy a toy, subtract it until you have **no more money** to spend.

25 ¢	−	4 ¢	=	21 ¢
21 ¢	−	___ ¢	=	___ ¢
___ ¢	−	___ ¢	=	___ ¢
___ ¢	−	___ ¢	=	___ ¢
___ ¢	−	___ ¢	=	___ ¢
___ ¢	−	___ ¢	=	___ ¢

Answers will vary.

One Step Further
What toy would you most like to buy for a friend?

Everyday Success First Grade

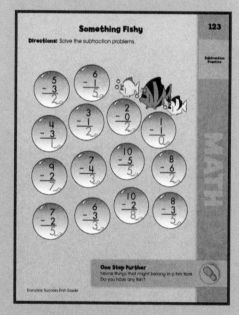

Something Fishy 123

Directions: Solve the subtraction problems.

$5 - 3 = 2$ 　 $6 - 1 = 5$

$4 - 3 = 1$ 　 $3 - 1 = 2$ 　 $2 - 2 = 0$ 　 $1 - 1 = 0$

$9 - 2 = 7$ 　 $7 - 4 = 3$ 　 $10 - 5 = 5$ 　 $8 - 6 = 2$

$7 - 2 = 5$ 　 $6 - 3 = 3$ 　 $10 - 2 = 8$ 　 $8 - 3 = 5$

One Step Further
Name things that might belong in a fish tank. Do you have any fish?

Everyday Success First Grade

A Swinging Adventure 124

Directions: Solve the subtraction problems.

$7 - 2 = 5$ 　 $6 - 3 = 3$ 　 $4 - 3 = 1$ 　 $3 - 2 = 1$

$10 - 7 = 3$ 　 $7 - 1 = 6$ 　 $10 - 1 = 9$ 　 $7 - 4 = 3$

$6 - 4 = 2$ 　 $8 - 4 = 4$ 　 $9 - 5 = 4$ 　 $8 - 1 = 7$ 　 $9 - 2 = 7$

$9 - 6 = 3$ 　 $5 - 4 = 1$ 　 $10 - 6 = 4$ 　 $7 - 3 = 4$ 　 $4 - 2 = 2$

$5 - 1 = 4$ 　 $9 - 5 = 4$ 　 $9 - 3 = 6$ 　 $8 - 5 = 3$ 　 $7 - 3 = 4$

One Step Further
Get with a friend and put on a play about Robin Hood.

Everyday Success First Grade

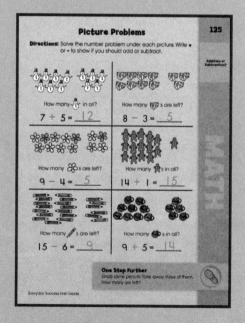

Picture Problems 125

Directions: Solve the number problem under each picture. Write + or − to show if you should add or subtract.

How many 🐧 in all?
$7 + 5 = \underline{12}$

How many 🦋s are left?
$8 - 3 = \underline{5}$

How many 🌼s are left?
$9 - 4 = \underline{5}$

How many 🌱s in all?
$14 + 1 = \underline{15}$

How many ✏️s are left?
$15 - 6 = \underline{9}$

How many 🫐s in all?
$9 + 5 = \underline{14}$

One Step Further
Grab some pencils. Take away three of them. How many are left?

Everyday Success First Grade

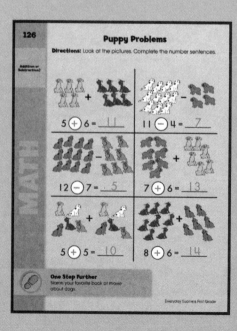

Puppy Problems 126

Directions: Look at the pictures. Complete the number sentences.

$5 + 6 = \underline{11}$ 　 $11 - 4 = \underline{7}$

$12 - 7 = \underline{5}$ 　 $7 + 6 = \underline{13}$

$5 + 5 = \underline{10}$ 　 $8 + 6 = \underline{14}$

One Step Further
Name your favorite book or movie about dogs.

Everyday Success First Grade

Everyday Success First Grade

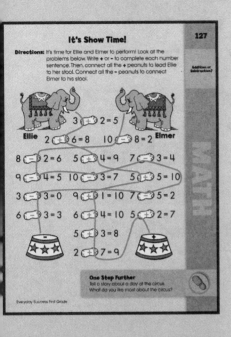

It's Show Time!

127

Addition or Subtraction?

Directions: It's time for Ellie and Elmer to perform! Look at the problems below. Write + or – to complete each number sentence. Then, connect all the + peanuts to lead Ellie to her stool. Connect all the – peanuts to connect Elmer to his stool.

Ellie 2 + 6 = 8   10 – 8 = 2 Elmer

3 – 2 = 5

8 – 2 = 6   5 + 4 = 9   7 – 3 = 4
9 – 4 = 5   10 – 3 = 7   5 + 5 = 10
3 – 3 = 0   9 + 1 = 10   7 – 5 = 2
6 – 3 = 3   6 + 4 = 10   5 – 2 = 7
5 + 3 = 8
2 + 7 = 9

One Step Further
Tell a story about a day at the circus. What do you like most about the circus?

Everyday Success First Grade

128

Addition or Subtraction?

Add or Subtract?

Directions: The key words "in all" tell you to add. The key word "left" tells you to subtract. Circle the key words and write + or – in the circles. Then, solve the problems.

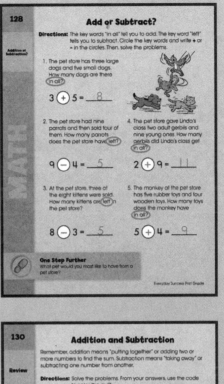

1. The pet store has three large dogs and five small dogs. How many dogs are there in all?

3 (+) 5 = 8

2. The pet store had nine parrots and then sold four of them. How many parrots does the pet store have left?

9 (–) 4 = 5

3. At the pet store, three of the eight kittens were sold. How many kittens are left in the pet store?

8 (–) 3 = 5

4. The pet store gave Linda's class two adult gerbils and nine young ones. How many gerbils did Linda's class get in all?

2 (+) 9 = 11

5. The monkey at the pet store has five rubber toys and four wooden toys. How many toys does the monkey have in all?

5 (+) 4 = 9

One Step Further
What pet would you most like to have from a pet store?

Everyday Success First Grade

Addition and Subtraction

129

Review

Directions: Solve the problems.

1 + 3 = 4   4 – 3 = 1   4 + 5 = 9

6 + 1 = 7   7 – 2 = 5   8 – 4 = 4

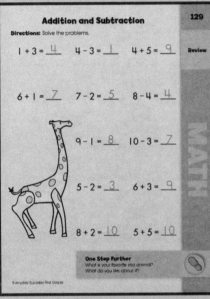

9 – 1 = 8   10 – 3 = 7

5 – 2 = 3   6 + 3 = 9

8 + 2 = 10   5 + 5 = 10

One Step Further
What is your favorite zoo animal? What do you like about it?

Everyday Success First Grade

130

Review

Addition and Subtraction

Remember, addition means "putting together" or adding two or more numbers to find the sum. Subtraction means "taking away" or subtracting one number from another.

Directions: Solve the problems. From your answers, use the code to color the quilt.

Color:
6 = blue
7 = yellow
8 = green
9 = red
10 = orange

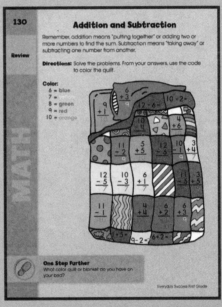

One Step Further
What color quilt or blanket do you have on your bed?

Everyday Success First Grade

Whole and Half

131

Fractions

A **fraction** is a number that names part of a whole, such as ½ or ⅓.

Directions: Color half of each object.

Example:

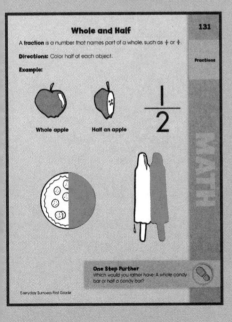

Whole apple   Half an apple $\frac{1}{2}$

One Step Further
Which would you rather have: A whole candy bar or half a candy bar?

Everyday Success First Grade

132

Fractions

Thirds

Directions: Circle the objects that have three equal parts.

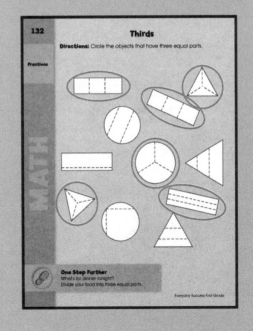

One Step Further
What's for dinner tonight? Divide your food into three equal parts.

Everyday Success First Grade

133 — Fourths

Fractions

Directions: Circle the objects that have four equal parts.

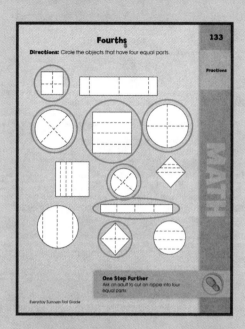

134 — Review

Fractions

Directions: Count the equal parts. Then, write the fraction.

Example:

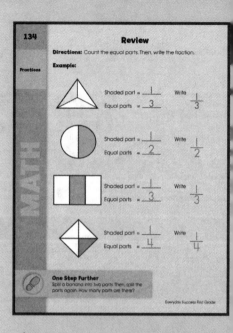

Shaded part = $\frac{1}{}$ Equal parts = $\frac{}{3}$ Write $\frac{1}{3}$

Shaded part = $\frac{1}{}$ Equal parts = $\frac{}{2}$ Write $\frac{1}{2}$

Shaded part = $\frac{1}{}$ Equal parts = $\frac{}{3}$ Write $\frac{1}{3}$

Shaded part = $\frac{1}{}$ Equal parts = $\frac{}{4}$ Write $\frac{1}{4}$

135 — Fractions

Fractions

One day, the monsters went to the pizza stand for a snack.

- Mug ate $\frac{1}{2}$ of a pizza.
- Lug ate $\frac{2}{4}$ of a pizza.
- Gug ate $\frac{3}{6}$ of a pizza.

Directions: Color the portion of pizza that each monster ate.

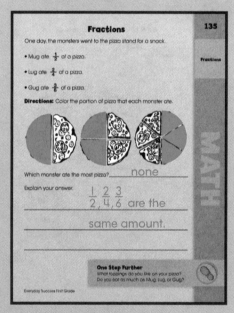

Which monster ate the most pizza? __none__

Explain your answer. $\frac{1}{2}, \frac{2}{4}, \frac{3}{6}$ are the same amount.

136 — Fractions

Fractions

Suji and Samantha had Millie and Milo over to play after school. Their mother gave them a plate of cookies to share. If they divide the cookies equally, how many cookies will there be for each monster?

Directions: Draw the cookies on the plates to show how many each monster gets.

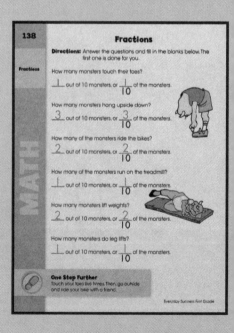

137 — Fractions

Fractions

The monsters are getting in shape.

Directions: Look below and on page 138 to see the different ways they are working out. Then, answer the questions on page 138.

138 — Fractions

Fractions

Directions: Answer the questions and fill in the blanks below. The first one is done for you.

How many monsters touch their toes?

$\frac{1}{}$ out of 10 monsters, or $\frac{1}{10}$ of the monsters.

How many monsters hang upside down?

$\frac{3}{}$ out of 10 monsters, or $\frac{3}{10}$ of the monsters.

How many of the monsters ride the bikes?

$\frac{2}{}$ out of 10 monsters, or $\frac{2}{10}$ of the monsters.

How many of the monsters run on the treadmill?

$\frac{1}{}$ out of 10 monsters, or $\frac{1}{10}$ of the monsters.

How many monsters lift weights?

$\frac{2}{}$ out of 10 monsters, or $\frac{2}{10}$ of the monsters.

How many monsters do leg lifts?

$\frac{1}{}$ out of 10 monsters, or $\frac{1}{10}$ of the monsters.

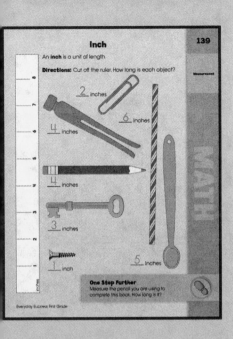

Inch
139

An **inch** is a unit of length.

Directions: Cut off the ruler. How long is each object?

_2_ inches

_6_ inches

_4_ inches

_4_ inches

_3_ inches

_1_ inch

_5_ inches

One Step Further
Measure the pencil you are using to complete this book. How long is it?

Everyday Success First Grade

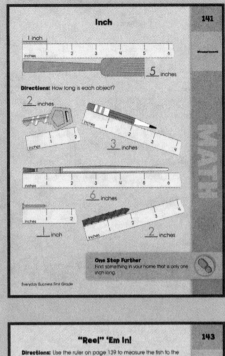

Inch
141

_1_ inch

_5_ inches

Directions: How long is each object?

_2_ inches

_3_ inches

_6_ inches

_1_ inch

_2_ inches

One Step Further
Find something in your home that is only one inch long.

Everyday Success First Grade

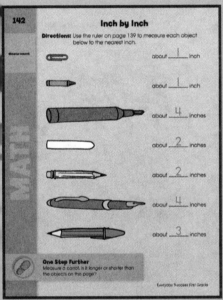

142

Inch by Inch

Directions: Use the ruler on page 139 to measure each object below to the nearest inch.

about _1_ inch

about _1_ inch

about _4_ inches

about _2_ inches

about _2_ inches

about _4_ inches

about _3_ inches

One Step Further
Measure a carrot. Is it longer or shorter than the objects on this page?

Everyday Success First Grade

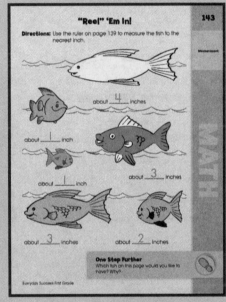

"Reel" 'Em In!
143

Directions: Use the ruler on page 139 to measure the fish to the nearest inch.

about _4_ inches

about _1_ inch

about _3_ inches

about _1_ inch

about _3_ inches

about _2_ inches

One Step Further
Which fish on this page would you like to have? Why?

Everyday Success First Grade

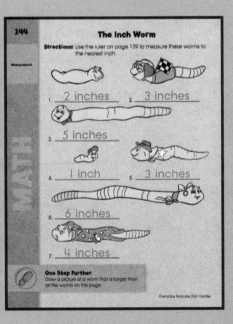

144

The Inch Worm

Directions: Use the ruler on page 139 to measure these worms to the nearest inch.

1. _2 inches_   2. _3 inches_

3. _5 inches_

4. _1 inch_   5. _3 inches_

6. _6 inches_

7. _4 inches_

One Step Further
Draw a picture of a worm that is longer than all the worms on this page.

Everyday Success First Grade

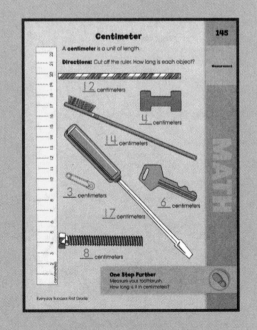

Centimeter
145

A **centimeter** is a unit of length.

Directions: Cut off the ruler. How long is each object?

_12_ centimeters

_4_ centimeters

_14_ centimeters

_3_ centimeters

_6_ centimeters

_17_ centimeters

_8_ centimeters

One Step Further
Measure your toothbrush. How long is it in centimeters?

Everyday Success First Grade

Centimeter 147

1 centimeter

_____ 11 centimeters

Directions: How long is each object?

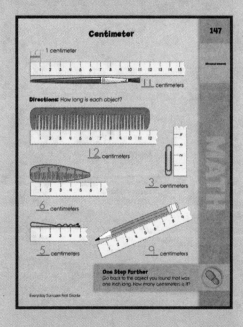

12 centimeters

3 centimeters

6 centimeters

5 centimeters

9 centimeters

One Step Further
Go back to the object you found that was one inch long. How many centimeters is it?

Everyday Success First Grade

---

148 Measuring

Work with a friend.

Directions: Use the centimeter ruler on page 145. Measure each other.

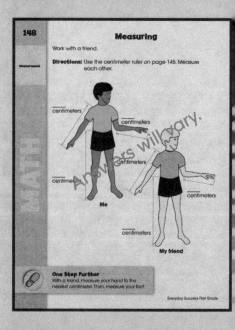

Answers will vary.

centimeters
centimeters
centimeters
centimeters
centimeters

Me

My friend

One Step Further
With a friend, measure your hand to the nearest centimeter. Then, measure your foot.

Everyday Success First Grade

Brush Up on Measuring! 149

Directions: Use the centimeter ruler on page 145 to measure these brushes to the nearest centimeter.

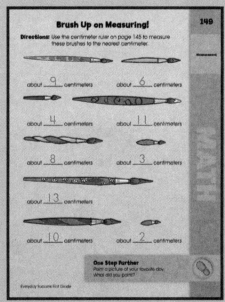

about 9 centimeters   about 6 centimeters

about 4 centimeters   about 11 centimeters

about 8 centimeters   about 3 centimeters

about 13 centimeters

about 10 centimeters   about 2 centimeters

One Step Further
Paint a picture of your favorite day. What did you paint?

Everyday Success First Grade

---

150 Flowers That "Measure" Up

Directions: Use the centimeter ruler on page 145 to measure how tall each flower is. Measure each flower from the bottom of the stem to the top of the flower. Write the answer on the blank by the flower.

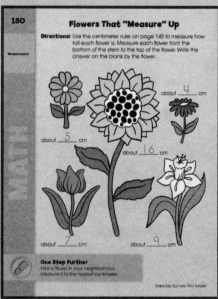

about 5 cm

about 16 cm

about 4

about 7 cm   about 9 cm

One Step Further
Find a flower in your neighborhood. Measure it to the nearest centimeter.

Everyday Success First Grade

How Far Is It? 151

Directions: Use the inch ruler on page 139 to measure each distance on the map. Then, use the letters on the circles and your answers to solve the message at the bottom of the page.

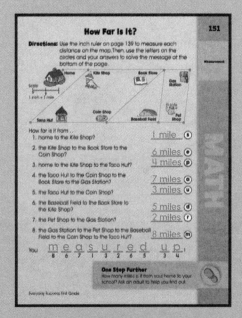

How far is it from . . .
1. home to the Kite Shop?   1 mile (s)
2. the Kite Shop to the Book Store to the Coin Shop?   6 miles (e)
3. home to the Kite Shop to the Taco Hut?   4 miles (p)
4. the Taco Hut to the Coin Shop to the Book Store to the Gas Station?   7 miles (a)
5. the Taco Hut to the Coin Shop?   3 miles (u)
6. the Baseball Field to the Book Store to the Kite Shop?   5 miles (d)
7. the Pet Shop to the Gas Station?   2 miles (r)
8. the Gas Station to the Pet Shop to the Baseball Field to the Coin Shop to the Taco Hut?   8 miles (m)

You   m e a s u r e d   u p !
      8 6 7 1 3 2 6 5   3 4

One Step Further
How many miles is it from your home to your school? Ask an adult to help you find out.

Everyday Success First Grade

---

152 Candy Graph

Directions: Make a **graph** using small colored candies. Put your candies in the correct column on the graphing mat below. Then, color each space on the graph to match the candy that you put on it. Answer the questions at the bottom of the page.

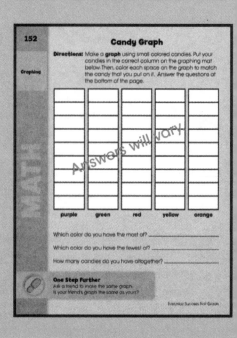

Answers will vary.

purple   green   red   yellow   orange

Which color do you have the most of? _____
Which color do you have the fewest of? _____
How many candies do you have altogether? _____

One Step Further
Ask a friend to make the same graph. Is your friend's graph the same as yours?

Everyday Success First Grade

Everyday Success First Grade

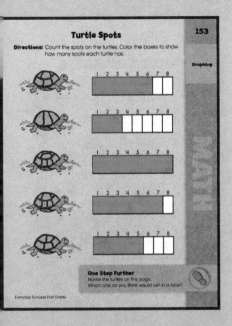

Turtle Spots 153

Directions: Count the spots on the turtles. Color the boxes to show how many spots each turtle has.

Graphing

One Step Further
Name the turtles on this page.
Which one do you think would win in a race?

Everyday Success First Grade

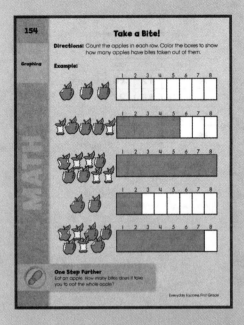

Take a Bite! 154

Graphing

Directions: Count the apples in each row. Color the boxes to show how many apples have bites taken out of them.

Example:

One Step Further
Eat an apple. How many bites does it take you to eat the whole apple?

Everyday Success First Grade

273

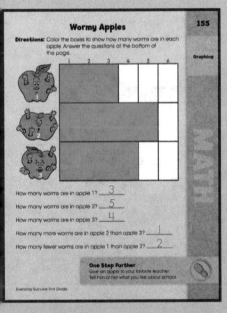

Wormy Apples 155

Directions: Color the boxes to show how many worms are in each apple. Answer the questions at the bottom of the page.

Graphing

How many worms are in apple 1? __3__

How many worms are in apple 2? __5__

How many worms are in apple 3? __4__

How many more worms are in apple 2 than apple 3? __1__

How many fewer worms are in apple 1 than apple 2? __2__

One Step Further
Give an apple to your favorite teacher.
Tell him or her what you like about school.

Everyday Success First Grade

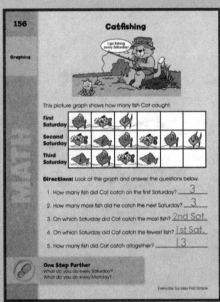

Catfishing 156

Graphing

This picture graph shows how many fish Cat caught.

First Saturday						
Second Saturday						
Third Saturday						

Directions: Look at the graph and answer the questions below.

1. How many fish did Cat catch on the first Saturday? __3__

2. How many more fish did he catch the next Saturday? __3__

3. On which Saturday did Cat catch the most fish? __2nd Sat.__

4. On which Saturday did Cat catch the fewest fish? __1st Sat.__

5. How many fish did Cat catch altogether? __13__

One Step Further
What do you do every Saturday?
What do you do every Monday?

Everyday Success First Grade

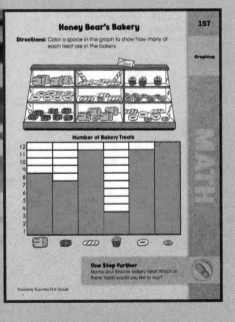

Honey Bear's Bakery 157

Directions: Color a space in the graph to show how many of each treat are in the bakery.

Graphing

Number of Bakery Treats

One Step Further
Name your favorite bakery treat. Which of these treats would you like to buy?

Everyday Success First Grade

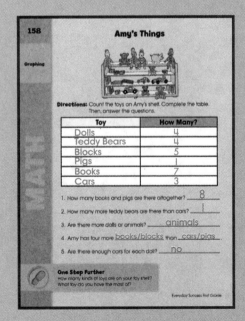

Amy's Things 158

Graphing

Directions: Count the toys on Amy's shelf. Complete the table. Then, answer the questions.

Toy	How Many?
Dolls	4
Teddy Bears	4
Blocks	5
Pigs	1
Books	7
Cars	3

1. How many books and pigs are there altogether? __8__

2. How many more teddy bears are there than cars? __1__

3. Are there more dolls or animals? __animals__

4. Amy has four more __books/blocks__ than __cars/pigs__

5. Are there enough cars for each doll? __no__

One Step Further
How many kinds of toys are on your toy shelf?
What toy do you have the most of?

Everyday Success First Grade

Everyday Success First Grade

Fantastic First Graders

Directions: Complete the table using the information shown. Then answer the questions.

Class	Boys	Girls	Total
A	11	17	28
B	12	15	27
C	9	14	23
Total	32	46	78

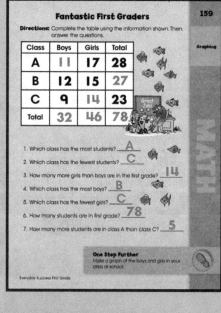

1. Which class has the most students? __A__
2. Which class has the fewest students? __C__
3. How many more girls than boys are in the first grade? __14__
4. Which class has the most boys? __B__
5. Which class has the fewest girls? __C__
6. How many students are in first grade? __78__
7. How many more students are in class A than class C? __5__

One Step Further
Make a graph of the boys and girls in your class at school.

Everyday Success First Grade

Food Fun

Directions: The table below tells what each animal brought to the picnic. Write the missing numbers.

Animal	Vegetables	Fruits	Total
Skunk	8	6	14
Raccoon	9	8	17
Squirrel	7	8	15
Rabbit	6	7	13
Owl	7	9	16
Deer	9	9	18

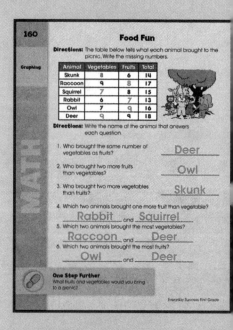

Directions: Write the name of the animal that answers each question.

1. Who brought the same number of vegetables as fruits? __Deer__
2. Who brought two more fruits than vegetables? __Owl__
3. Who brought two more vegetables than fruits? __Skunk__
4. Which two animals brought one more fruit than vegetable? __Rabbit__ and __Squirrel__
5. Which two animals brought the most vegetables? __Raccoon__ and __Deer__
6. Which two animals brought the most fruits? __Owl__ and __Deer__

One Step Further
What fruits and vegetables would you bring to a picnic?

Everyday Success First Grade

Graphing

Make your own graph.

Here is a happy face:

Here is a sad face:

Directions: Count up the happy and sad faces you see below. Then, answer the questions.

How many happy faces did you count? __5__
How many sad faces did you count? __4__
How many faces are there in all? __9__

One Step Further
Take a picture of yourself making a happy face.

Everyday Success First Grade

Graphing

Directions: Now, make a graph of the happy and sad faces you counted on page 161. The first row has been done for you. A happy face and a sad face have been drawn in. Fill in the other rows to complete the graph.

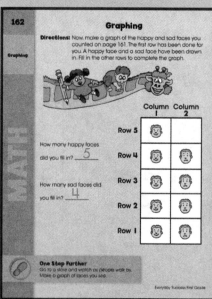

How many happy faces did you fill in? __5__

How many sad faces did you fill in? __4__

	Column 1	Column 2
Row 5	😊	
Row 4	😊	😊
Row 3	😊	😊
Row 2	😊	😊
Row 1	😊	😊

One Step Further
Go to a store and watch as people walk by. Make a graph of faces you see.

Everyday Success First Grade

Graphing

It's a birthday party! There are lots of good foods to eat.

Directions: Count up all the foods you see.

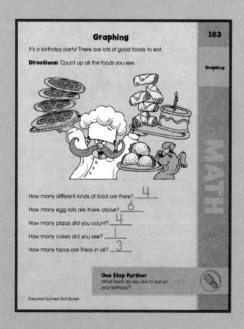

How many different kinds of food are there? __4__
How many egg rolls are there above? __6__
How many pizzas did you count? __4__
How many cakes did you see? __1__
How many tacos are there in all? __3__

One Step Further
What foods do you like to eat on your birthday?

Everyday Success First Grade

Graphing

Directions: Complete the graph below. Use the number of each animal you counted to fill in the rows with the missing pictures of turtles and dogs. The giraffes and sheep have been filled in for you.

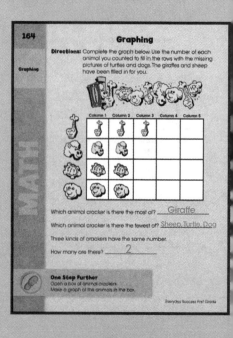

Which animal cracker is there the most of? __Giraffe__

Which animal cracker is there the fewest of? __Sheep, Turtle, Dog__

Three kinds of crackers have the same number.

How many are there? __2__

One Step Further
Open a box of animal crackers. Make a graph of the animals in the box.

Everyday Success First Grade

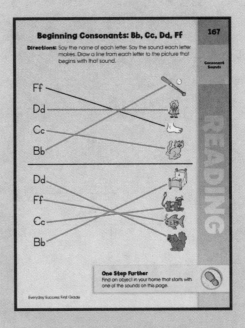

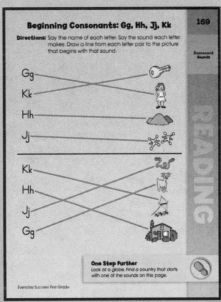

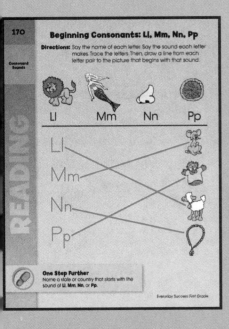

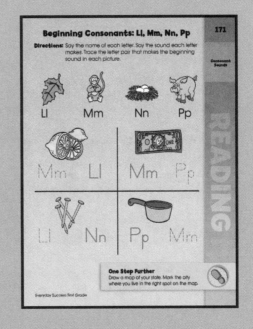

Everyday Success First Grade

ANSWER KEY

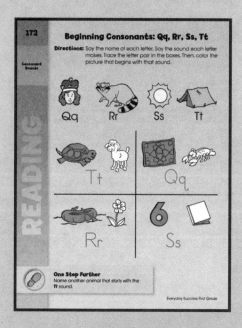

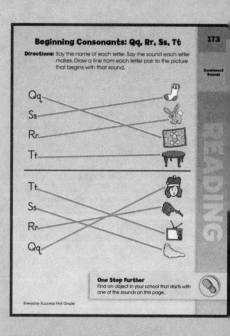

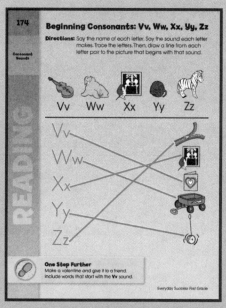

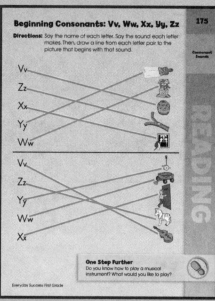

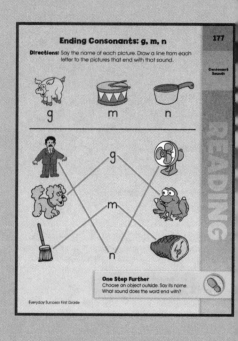

178

Ending Consonants: k, l, p

Directions: Trace the letters in each row. Say the name of each picture. Then, color the pictures in each row that end with that sound.

k

l

p

One Step Further
How many of the objects on this page can you find in your home?

Everyday Success First Grade

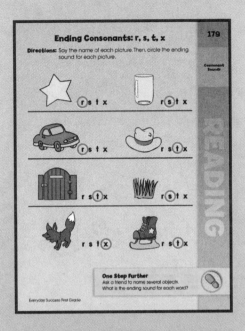

179

Ending Consonants: r, s, t, x

Directions: Say the name of each picture. Then, circle the ending sound for each picture.

r (s) t x   r (s) t x

r (s) t x   r s (t) x

r (s) t x   r s (t) x

r s t (x)   r s (t) x

One Step Further
Ask a friend to name several objects. What is the ending sound for each word?

Everyday Success First Grade

180

Consonant Review

Directions: One letter is missing in each word. Write the missing letter on the line.

dog   box   sun

hen   tulip   top

log   leaf   wagon

One Step Further
Draw a picture of something in your home. Write the name of the object you drew.

Everyday Success First Grade

181

Consonant Review

Directions: Write all the missing consonants.

man   fox   pig

bed   jar   camel

goat   car   cap

One Step Further
What state do you live in? Which consonants are in the name of your state?

Everyday Success First Grade

182

Meet Short a

Listen for the sound of short **a** in **van**.

van

Directions: Trace the letter. Write it on the line.

A A A A A A A

a a a a a a a a

Directions: Color the pictures whose names have the short **a** sound.

One Step Further
How many words can you name that rhyme with **cat**? Do they have the short **a** sound?

Everyday Success First Grade

183

Short a Maze

Directions: Help the cat get to the bag. Connect all the pictures whose names have the short **a** sound from the cat to the bag.

One Step Further
Draw more objects that have the short **a** sound.

Everyday Success First Grade

ANSWER KEY

184

Meet Short e

Listen for the sound of short **e** in **hen**.

Directions: Trace the letter. Write it on the line.

E E E E E E E

e e e e e e e

Directions: Color the pictures whose names have the short **e** sound.

One Step Further
Tell a story about a hen. What words in your story have the short **e** sound?

Everyday Success First Grade

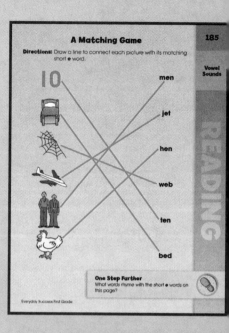

A Matching Game

185

Directions: Draw a line to connect each picture with its matching short **e** word.

men

jet

hen

web

ten

bed

One Step Further
What words rhyme with the short **e** words on this page?

Everyday Success First Grade

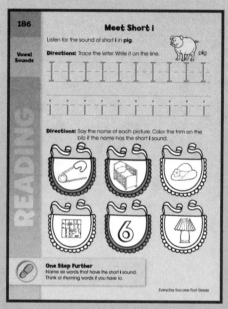

186

Meet Short i

Listen for the sound of short **i** in **pig**.

Directions: Trace the letter. Write it on the line.

I I I I I I I

i i i i i i i

Directions: Say the name of each picture. Color the trim on the bib if the name has the short **i** sound.

One Step Further
Name six words that have the short **i** sound. Think of rhyming words if you have to.

Everyday Success First Grade

Read and Color Short i

187

Directions: Say the name of each picture. Color the pictures whose names have the short **i** sound. The words in the box will give you hints.

| milk | crib | bib |
| pig | kitten | fish |

One Step Further
Tell a story about what is happening in the picture.

Everyday Success First Grade

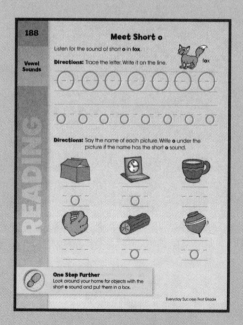

188

Meet Short o

Listen for the sound of short **o** in **fox**.

Directions: Trace the letter. Write it on the line.

O O O O O O O

o o o o o o o

Directions: Say the name of each picture. Write **o** under the picture if the name has the short **o** sound.

One Step Further
Look around your home for objects with the short **o** sound and put them in a box.

Everyday Success First Grade

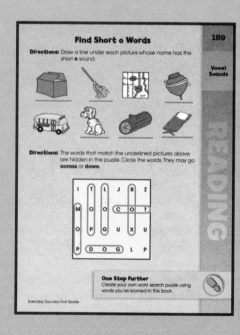

Find Short o Words

189

Directions: Draw a line under each picture whose name has the short **o** sound.

Directions: The words that match the underlined pictures above are hidden in this puzzle. Circle the words. They may go **across** or **down**.

One Step Further
Create your own word search puzzle using words you've learned in this book.

Everyday Success First Grade

Everyday Success First Grade

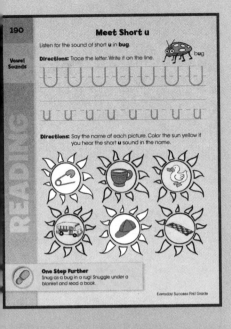

190

Vowel Sounds

Meet Short u

Listen for the sound of short **u** in **bug**.

Directions: Trace the letter. Write it on the line.

bug

U U U U U U U U

u u u u u u u u

Directions: Say the name of each picture. Color the sun yellow if you hear the short **u** sound in the name.

One Step Further
Snug as a bug in a rug! Snuggle under a blanket and read a book.

Everyday Success First Grade

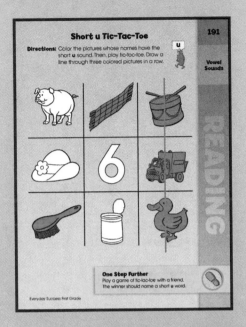

191

Vowel Sounds

Short u Tic-Tac-Toe

Directions: Color the pictures whose names have the short **u** sound. Then, play tic-tac-toe. Draw a line through three colored pictures in a row.

One Step Further
Play a game of tic-tac-toe with a friend. The winner should name a short **u** word.

192

Vowel Sounds

Meet Long a

Listen for the sound of long **a** in **cake**.

Directions: Color the pictures whose names have the long **a** sound.

cake

One Step Further
What vowels does your name contain? Are they long or short vowels?

Everyday Success First Grade

193

Vowel Sounds

Meet Long e

Listen for the sound of long **e** in **bee**. The letters **ee** and **ea** usually stand for the long **e** sound.

Directions: Write the name of the picture on the correct line.

bee

seal   ten   beet   jeep   leaf

bed   red   seat   feet

ee	**ea**	**Short Vowel e**
beet	seal	ten
jeep	leaf	bed
feet	seat	red

One Step Further
Can you think of other words that contain the long **e** sound?

Everyday Success First Grade

194

Vowel Sounds

Meet Long i

Listen for the sound of long **i** in **bike**. Look for **i_e**.

Directions: Fill in the circle beside the name of the picture.

bike

- ○ dim
- ○ date
- ● dime

- ● five
- ○ fix
- ○ fame

- ● kite
- ○ cat
- ○ kit

- ○ pane
- ○ pin
- ● pine

- ○ tin
- ● tire
- ○ tale

- ○ red
- ● ride
- ○ rid

- ● hive
- ○ hid
- ○ had

- ○ nip
- ○ name
- ● nine

- ● fame
- ○ fire
- ○ tin

One Step Further
What words rhyme with the words you circled? Do they have the short **i** sound, too?

Everyday Success First Grade

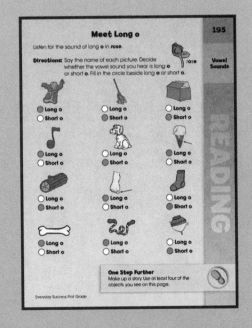

195

Vowel Sounds

Meet Long o

Listen for the sound of long **o** in **rose**.

Directions: Say the name of each picture. Decide whether the vowel sound you hear is long **o** or short **o**. Fill in the circle beside long **o** or short **o**.

rose

- ● Long o
- ○ Short o

- ○ Long o
- ● Short o

- ● Long o
- ○ Short o

- ● Long o
- ○ Short o

- ○ Long o
- ● Short o

- ● Long o
- ○ Short o

- ○ Long o
- ● Short o

- ○ Long o
- ● Short o

- ○ Long o
- ● Short o

- ● Long o
- ○ Short o

- ● Long o
- ○ Short o

- ○ Long o
- ● Short o

One Step Further
Make up a story. Use at least four of the objects you see on this page.

Everyday Success First Grade

ANSWER KEY